T0283596

Internet Infrastructure

Internet Infrastructure

Liliana Cooper

Larsen & Keller
www.larsen-keller.com

Internet Infrastructure
Liliana Cooper
ISBN: 978-1-64172-099-1 (Hardback)

 Larsen & Keller

Published by Larsen and Keller Education,
5 Penn Plaza,
19th Floor,
New York, NY 10001, USA

Cataloging-in-Publication Data

Internet infrastructure / Liliana Cooper.
    p. cm.
Includes bibliographical references and index.
ISBN 978-1-64172-099-1
1. Internet. 2. Internetworking (Telecommunication). 3. Web services. I. Cooper, Liliana.
TK5105.875.I57 I58 2019
004.678--dc23

For more information regarding Larsen and Keller Education and its products, please visit the publisher's website www.larsen-keller.com

Table of Contents

Preface

The Internet infrastructure or the communications infrastructure of the Internet comprises of its various hardware and software components that control the varied aspects of computer architecture. It encompasses various components for routing and data exchange, Internet access, protocols, etc. Wired, microwave and fiber optic links along with varied equipment for routing are responsible for the transmission of data. Website hosting, the Domain Name System (DNS), Email, database servers, authentication and authorization, and storage systems, etc. are critical software services that are part of Internet infrastructure. This book is a compilation of chapters that discuss the most vital concepts in the field of Internet infrastructure. Such selected concepts that redefine this field have been presented in this book. It attempts to assist those with a goal of delving into the field of Internet infrastructure.

To facilitate a deeper understanding of the contents of this book a short introduction of every chapter is written below:

Chapter 1, Internet infrastructure refers to all software and hardware systems that together comprise the requisite components in the operation of the Internet. This chapter has been carefully written to provide an introduction to Internet infrastructure and discusses the essentials of internet and internet infrastructure. **Chapter 2**, A computer or data network is a system of digital telecommunication, which facilitates the exchange of resources across nodes. The topics elucidated in this chapter provide an insight into this field through the elucidation of the varied types of computer networks such as LAN, WAN, PAN, WLAN, etc. **Chapter 3**, Network infrastructure comprises of the essential elements of network nodes such as network interfaces, repeaters and hubs, switches, bridges, modems, routers, etc. Apart from this, it comprises of network links and network structure elements. This chapter closely examines the vital aspects of network infrastructure and includes topics such as firewalls, servers, gateways, proxies, among many others. **Chapter 4**, The Internet protocol suite refers to a set of communications protocols that is used on computer networks and the Internet. Some of the varied topics covered in this chapter include OSI reference model, TCP/IP model, application layer, transport layer, internet layer, etc. for a detailed understanding of internet protocol suite. **Chapter 5**, The Domain Name System, or the DNS, is a centralized naming system for entities like computers, services, etc. that are connected to a private network or to the Internet. Some of the significant aspects of DNS, such as dynamic DNS, extension mechanisms for DNS, DNS blocking, DNS hijacking, reverse DNS lookup, etc. have been covered for an extensive understanding. **Chapter 6**, An Internet exchange point is the infrastructure that allows the exchange of Internet traffic to content delivery networks and Internet service providers between their networks. Some of the concepts fundamental to the understanding of Internet Exchange Point are commercial Internet exchange and federal Internet exchange, which have been extensively discussed in this chapter.

Chapter 7, Web server is the server software or the hardware that is dedicated to the delivery of content to the World Wide Web. It involves the processing of network requests over HTTP. An understanding of web servers, hypertext transfer protocol, HTTP header fields and status codes, web cache and security access control methods is required for an understanding of Internet infrastructure. This chapter extensively covers these topics for a detailed understanding. **Chapter 8**, A proxy server is a computer system which works as an intermediary for handling requests from clients desiring resources from other servers. This is an important chapter, which will analyze in detail about the different proxy servers such as open proxy server, reverse proxy server, flash proxy, Java Anon proxy server, etc.

I would like to share the credit of this book with my editorial team who worked tirelessly on this book. I owe the completion of this book to the never-ending support of my family, who supported me throughout the project.

Liliana Cooper

Introduction to Internet Infrastructure

Internet infrastructure refers to all software and hardware systems that together comprise the requisite components in the operation of the Internet. This chapter has been carefully written to provide an introduction to Internet infrastructure and discusses the essentials of internet and internet infrastructure.

The Internet, sometimes called simply "the Net," is a worldwide system of computer networks - a network of networks in which users at any one computer can, if they have permission, get information from any other computer (and sometimes talk directly to users at other computers). It was conceived by the Advanced Research Projects Agency (ARPA) of the U.S. government in 1969 and was first known as the ARPANET. The original aim was to create a network that would allow users of a research computer at one university to "talk to" research computers at other universities. A side benefit of ARPANET's design was that, because messages could be routed or rerouted in more than one direction, the network could continue to function even if parts of it were destroyed in the event of a military attack or other disaster.

Today, the Internet is a public, cooperative and self-sustaining facility accessible to hundreds of millions of people worldwide. Physically, the Internet uses a portion of the total resources of the currently existing public telecommunication networks. Technically, what distinguishes the Internet is its use of a set of protocols called TCP/IP (for Transmission Control Protocol/Internet Protocol). Two recent adaptations of Internet technology, the intranet and the extranet, also make use of the TCP/IP protocol.

For most Internet users, electronic mail (email) practically replaced the postal service for short written transactions. People communicate over the Internet in a number of other ways including Internet Relay Chat (IRC), Internet telephony, instant messaging, video chat or social media.

The most widely used part of the Internet is the World Wide Web (often abbreviated "WWW" or called "the Web"). Its outstanding feature is hypertext, a method of instant cross-referencing. In most Web sites, certain words or phrases appear in text of a different color than the rest; often this text is also underlined. When you select one of these words or phrases, you will be transferred to the site or page that is relevant to this word or phrase. Sometimes there are buttons, images, or portions of images that are "clickable." If you move the pointer over a spot on a Web site and the pointer changes into a hand, this indicates that you can click and be transferred to another site.

Using the Web, you have access to billions of pages of information. Web browsing is done with a Web browser, the most popular of which are Chrome, Firefox and Internet Explorer. The appearance of a particular Web site may vary slightly depending on the browser you use. Also, later versions of a particular browser are able to render more "bells and whistles" such as animation, virtual reality, sound, and music files, than earlier versions.

The Internet has continued to grow and evolve over the years of its existence. IPv6, for example, was designed to anticipate enormous future expansion in the number of available IP addresses. In a related development, the Internet of Things (IoT) is the burgeoning environment in which almost any entity or object can be provided with a unique identifier and the ability to transfer data automatically over the Internet.

Society and The Internet

What began as a largely technical and limited universe of designers and users became one of the most important mediums of the late 20th and early 21st centuries. As the Pew Charitable Trust observed in 2004, it took 46 years to wire 30 percent of the United States for electricity; it took only 7 years for the Internet to reach that same level of connection to American homes. By 2005, 68 percent of American adults and 90 percent of American teenagers had used the Internet. Europe and Asia were at least as well connected as the United States. Nearly half of the citizens of the European Union are online, and even higher rates are found in the Scandinavian countries. There is a wide variance in Asian countries; for example, by 2005 Taiwan, Hong Kong, and Japan had at least half of their populations online, whereas India, Pakistan, and Vietnam had less than 10 percent. South Korea was the world leader in connecting its population to the Internet through high-speed broadband connections.

Internet: effect on language Learn about the Internet and its effect on verbal communication.

Such statistics can chart the Internet's growth, but they offer few insights into the changes wrought as users—individuals, groups, corporations, and governments—have embedded the technology into everyday life. The Internet is now as much a lived experience as a tool for performing particular tasks, offering the possibility of creating an environment or virtual reality in which individuals might work, socially interact with others, and perhaps even live out their lives.

Instant Broadcast Communication

For the individual, the Internet opened up new communication possibilities. E-mail led to a substantial decline in traditional "snail mail." Instant messaging (IM), or text messaging, expanded, especially among youth, with the convergence of the Internet and cellular telephone access to the Web. Indeed, IM became a particular problem in classrooms, with students often surreptitiously exchanging notes via wireless communication devices. More than 50 million American adults, including 11 million at work, use IM.

From mailing lists to "buddy lists," e-mail and IM have been used to create "smart mobs" that converge in the physical world. Examples include protest organizing, spontaneous performance art, and shopping. Obviously, people congregated before the Internet existed, but the change wrought by mass e-mailings was in the speed of assembling such events. In February 1999, for example, activists began planning protests against the November 1999 World Trade Organization (WTO) meetings in Seattle, Washington. Using the Internet, organizers mobilized more than 50,000 individuals from around the world to engage in demonstrations—at times violent—that effectively altered the WTO's agenda.

More than a decade later, in June 2010 Egyptian computer engineer Wael Ghonim anonymously created a page titled "We Are All Khaled Said" on the social media site Facebook to publicize the death of a 28-year-old Egyptian man beaten to death by police. The page garnered hundreds of thousands of members, becoming an online forum for the discussion of police brutality in Egypt. After a popular uprising in Tunisia in January 2011, Ghonim and several other Internet democracy activists posted messages to their sites calling for similar action in Egypt. Their social media campaign helped spur mass demonstrations that forced Egyptian Pres. Ḥosnī Mubārak from power.

In the wake of catastrophic disasters, citizens have used the Internet to donate to charities in an unprecedented fashion. Others have used the Internet to reunite family members or to match lost pets with their owners. The role of the Internet in responding to disasters, both natural and deliberate, remains the topic of much discussion, as it is unclear whether the Internet actually can function in a disaster area when much of the infrastructure is destroyed. Certainly during the September 11, 2001, attacks, people found it easier to communicate with loved ones in New York City via e-mail than through the overwhelmed telephone network.

Following the earthquake that struck Haiti in January 2010, electronic media emerged as a useful mode for connecting those separated by the quake and for coordinating relief efforts. Survivors who were able to access the Internet—and friends and relatives abroad—took to social networking sites such as Facebook in search of information on those missing in the wake of the catastrophe. Feeds from those sites also assisted aid organizations in constructing maps of the areas affected and in determining where to channel resources. The many Haitians lacking Internet access were able to contribute updates via text messaging on mobile phones.

Social Gaming and Social Networking

One-to-one or even one-to-many communication is only the most elementary form of Internet social life. The very nature of the Internet makes spatial distances largely irrelevant for social interactions. Online gaming moved from simply playing a game with friends to a rather complex form of social life in which the game's virtual reality spills over into the physical world. The case of World of Warcraft, a popular electronic game with several million players, is one example. Property acquired in the game can be sold online, although such secondary economies are discouraged by Blizzard Entertainment, the publisher of World of Warcraft, as a violation of the game's terms of service. In any case, what does it mean that one can own virtual property and that someone is willing to pay for this property with real money? Economists have begun studying such virtual economies, some of which now exceed the gross national product of countries in Africa and Asia. In fact, virtual economies have given economists a means of running controlled experiments.

Millions of people have created online game characters for entertainment purposes. Gaming creates an online community, but it also allows for a blurring of the boundaries between the real world and the virtual one. In Shanghai one gamer stabbed and killed another one in the real world over a virtual sword used in Legend of Mir 3. Although attempts were made to involve the authorities in the original dispute, the police found themselves at a loss prior to the murder because the law did not acknowledge the existence of virtual property. In South Korea violence surrounding online gaming happens often enough that police refer to such murders as "off-line PK," a reference to player killing (PK), or player-versus-player lethal contests, which are allowed or encouraged in some games. By 2001 crime related to Lineage had forced South Korean police to create special cybercrime units to patrol both within the game and off-line. Potential problems from such games are not limited to crime. Virtual life can be addictive. Reports of players neglecting family, school, work, and even their health to the point of death have become more common.

Social networking sites (SNSs) emerged as a significant online phenomenon since the bursting of the "Internet bubble" in the early 2000s. SNSs use software to facilitate online communities where members with shared interests swap files, photographs, videos, and music, send messages and chat, set up blogs (Web diaries) and discussion groups, and share opinions. Early social networking services included Classmates.com, which connected former schoolmates, and Yahoo! 360° and Six-Degrees, which built networks of connections via friends of friends. In the post bubble era the leading social networking services were Myspace, Facebook, Friendster, Orkut, and LinkedIn. LinkedIn became an effective tool for business staff recruiting. Businesses have begun to exploit these networks, drawing on social networking research and theory, which suggests that finding key "influential" members of existing networks of individuals can give those businesses access to and credibility with the whole network.

Advertising and E-commerce

Nichification allows for consumers to find what they want, but it also provides opportunities for advertisers to find consumers. For example, most search engines generate revenue by matching ads to an individual's particular search query. Among the greatest challenges facing the Internet's continued development is the task of reconciling advertising and commercial needs with the right of Internet users not to be bombarded by "pop-up" Web pages and spam (unsolicited e-mail).

Nichification also opens up important e-commerce opportunities. A bookstore can carry only so much inventory on its shelves, which thereby limits its collection to books with broad appeal. An online bookstore can "display" nearly everything ever published. Although traditional bookstores often have a special-order department, consumers have taken to searching and ordering from online stores from the convenience of their homes and offices.

Although books can be made into purely digital artifacts, "e-books" have not sold nearly as well as digital music. In part, this disparity is due to the need for an e-book reader to have a large, bright screen, which adds to the display's cost and weight and leads to more-frequent battery replacement. Also, it is difficult to match the handy design and low cost of an old-fashioned paperback book. Interestingly, it turns out that listeners download from online music vendors as many obscure songs as big record company hits. Just a few people interested in some obscure song are enough to make it worthwhile for a vendor to store it electronically for sale over the Internet. What makes the Internet special here is not only its ability to match buyers and sellers quickly and relatively inexpensively but also that the Internet and the digital economy in general allow for a flowering of multiple tastes—in games, people, and music.

Internet Access

Internet access is the process of connecting to the internet using personal computers, laptops or mobile devices by users or enterprises. Internet access is subject to data signalling rates and users could be connected at different internet speeds. Internet access enables individuals or organizations to avail internet services/web-based services.

There are two access methods direct and Indirect and these can be either fixed or mobile.

Indirect Access

This is most common method used in home and office networks.

The device e.g. computer connects to a network using Ethernet or WiFi and the network connects to the Internet using ADSL, cable or fibre.

Direct Access

This is most common method used when traveling.

The device e.g. smart phone connects directly to the Internet using 3G/4G mobile networks or public Wi-Fi.

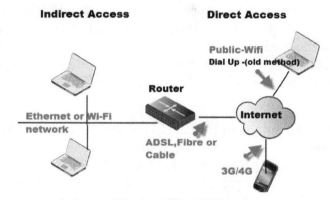

Internet Connection Methods

Fixed Internet- Home/Office

Fixed access is usually much faster and reliable than mobile, and is used for connecting homes/offices. The main Access mechanisms are:

- ADSL over traditional Phone Lines (most common).
- Cable (limited to cable TV areas).
- Fibre broadband – Currently being rolled out.

Pros

- Very Fast and reliable.
- Good for streaming video.
- Cheap when compared to Mobile.

- Can easily share the connection.

Cons

- Requires a fixed connection.
- Not usable when at a remote location.
- Fixed access is the most common way that businesses and home uses use for connecting to the Internet.

Mobile Internet

When traveling away from the fixed location mobile access is used.

Mobile Internet tends to be mainly a secondary access mechanism. The main access methods are:

- Mobile broadband over 3G Network (common but slow) or 4G.
- Public/ Private Wii-FI (common).

Pros

- No fixed connection required.
- Available from remote locations.

Cons

- Not as Fast and reliable as Fixed Access.
- Not good for streaming video.
- Expensive.
- Can't easily share the connection.

ADSL Broadband over Existing Phone Lines

This is probably the most common way to connect to the Internet for home and small business users.

Connection to the Internet for home/home offices is usually accomplished with ADSL (Asymmetric digital subscriber line) which uses the existing telephone cabling infrastructure.

In the UK BT (British Telecom) provide the familiar telephone connection to most homes, and these same telephone wires are used to provide broadband internet using ADSL technology.

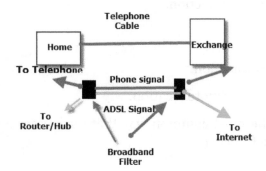

ADSL Over Phone Lines

It is the job of the broadband filter to split the phone signal from the broadband signal.

A filter must be installed on a telephone extension that has a telephone connected.

The Internet Signal from the filter is feed into a broadband router/Hub which can be used to form a home network.

BT provide their own broadband services using these telephone lines, and must also provide access to these lines to third party providers.

Other providers that utilize these BT lines are:

- SKY broadband
- Talk Talk broadband
- Virgin National Broadband

Broadband speeds quoted by providers are the maximum that is possible over an ADSL connection, and the speed you actually get depends mainly on how far you are from the local telephone exchange.

Cable Broadband

Cable connects you to the Internet through a coaxial cable usually using the same line as your TV service. Cable connections offer very high connection speeds, but the connection may be shared with other users. This means that you can experience much slower speeds due to congestion. In the UK Virgin Media are the only suppliers of cable broadband, which they market as fibre broadband. However it is not fibre all the way to the home but fibre to the cabinet, as the last part of the connection utilises the old coaxial cable connections.

Despite this download speeds of up to 152Mbs are being offered on broadband packages.

Fibre or Fiber Broadband

This is currently being rolled out in the UK by BT, and offers download speeds of 76Mbit/s.

BT offers two types depending on your location:

- Fibre to Home
- Fibre to Cabinet

Fibre to the home is the fastest and means that the connection from the home to the exchange is all fibre. This service require new hardware.

Fibre to the cabinet is slower than fibre to the home as the entire connection isn't fibre but only the connection from the exchange to the street cabinet.

In the diagram below cable section 1 is fibre and cable section 2 is twisted pair copper cable (old telephone lines).

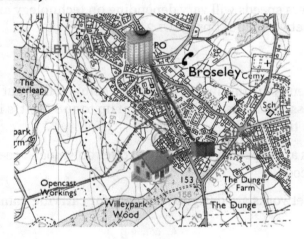

Other UK Providers

- Just as with ADSL broadband other operators have access to the BT fibre network and will offer fibre services that use the BT infrastructure.
- Virgin Media are the only other UK provider of fibre connections.
- Although probably not as common as ADSL this is the best way to connect to the Internet if it is available in your area.

Mobile Broadband 3G and 4G

- 3G and 4G networks are provided by mobile phone operators.
- 3G mobile phone networks are the most common, and have the widest coverage

area, whereas the newer 4G networks are less common with restricted coverage area.

- Mobile Internet services are available on a contract or pay as you go basis.

3G Broadband

- 3G mobile networks were designed mainly for phone calls (voice) but with improved internet access speeds when compared to the earlier 2G standard.

- A 3G mobile phone can make voice calls, and also access the Internet using a data channel.

- Mobile phone operators usually have two separate plans – standard voice plans and a data plan.

- Data plans tend to have restricted download limits and exceeding them can be expensive.

- Internet access speeds will vary depending on technology and location, but you can expect between 200kbps and 7.2Mbps.

4G Broadband

- This is currently in the initial phases of being rolled out in the UK. It uses HSPA+ access mechanism with speeds of up to 168 Mbit/s in the downlink and 22 Mbit/s in the uplink.

- 4G networks are expected eventually to offer download speeds of up to 1Gbits/s (LTE advanced).

- 4G mobile networks are designed primary for carrying data using the IP protocol.

- Capability is already built into Google Nexus 7 (mobile data model) and the Nexus 4 mobile phone.

  Due to the excellent speed potential 4G networks may replace fixed line networks in some rural areas.

  In developing countries and new build areas it could become the main connection type.

Public Wi-Fi -Wireless Broadband

The wireless technology used is the same as is used in home wireless networking, and hence if you have laptop/pda that is equipped for connection to a home or office wireless network then it will also work on a public wireless network.

The problem with this is that it is available only in limited areas usually public areas like airports, train stations etc., and it poses a very strong security risk see.

Old Methods- Not Really used any more

These types of access date back to the early days of the Internet, and may no longer be provided by most ISPs.

Dial-Up Analogue Connection -56K

Monthly Cost: Varies from 1p per minute to £13 per month (unlimited access).

Speed: Up to 56Kbps

Hardware Requirements: 56k modem included in most modern PCs (approx. £25-£50).

Advantages	Disadvantages
Inexpensive	Using a modem ties up a phone line.
	Connection is not "always on".
Wide availability	Slowest access method.
	Security danger see rogue Internet dialers.

Suitability

Basic Internet browsing and email. Not suitable if regularly downloading or uploading large files like music, video or pictures.

Internet Infrastructure

Generally speaking, infrastructures are the frameworks or architectures that systems are made of. For example, a nation's transportation infrastructure consists of roadways, railroads, airports, ocean ports, and rivers. Although not as visible to the naked eye, the Internet also has an infrastructure consisting of many different elements, each of which plays a critical role in the delivery of information from one point to another.

Elements of The Internet Infrastructure

At the most rudimentary level of the Internet infrastructure are endless miles of telephone lines and fiber optic cable. These cables connect millions of individual users and businesses to other parties, transmitting data at varying speeds, depending on the types of cabling used. Another factor that affects the speed and quality of a user's connection is the means of connection, which include telephone modems; high-speed connection methods like cable modems, ISDN, DSL, and T1 lines; and company networks.

According to the Strategis Group, high-speed residential Internet service was expected to surpass telephone dialup methods in the United States by 2005, at which time Strategis predicted there would be 36 million broadband subscribers.

It's easier to understanding how pieces of the Internet infrastructure work if one visualizes them transmitting data. The first step involved in sending or receiving data involves ISPs, which maintain racks upon racks of modems. Users connect to these modems in order to gain access to the ISP's network, which can vary in reach depending on the ISP's size. In the early 2000s, there were more than 7,000 ISPs throughout the world. The top 10 accounted for only 25 percent of total Internet access traffic. Once connected to an ISP, users then attempt to communicate by sending e-mail messages to other Internet users or by requesting Web pages or downloadable files from any number of servers located across the world. Servers are the computers used by individuals, companies, and other organizations to host Web sites, e-mail systems, or files that can be downloaded.

The process used to send and receive information across the world is more or less hidden to the user, and occurs in just seconds. In order for this to happen, a user on one ISP's network must be able to connect to users on another ISP's network, which may be located across the nation or across the globe. An exception to this would be if two users were located on the same ISP's network. ISPs connect to one another at NAPs, also called Internet exchanges (IX), which are major pieces of the Internet's backbone.

When the NSF opened the Internet to commercial enterprises in 1995, the first NAPs were located in Chicago; Pennsauken, New Jersey; Washington, D.C.; and San Francisco. These were operated by Ameritech, Sprint, Pac Bell, and MFS (a predecessor of MCI WorldCom). MFS later created two coastal access points called metropolitan area exchanges (MAE). By the early 2000s, there were more than 10 major access points throughout the United States. Sometimes ISPs make arrangements to establish direct connections between their networks. Known as private peering, this eliminates the need for relying on one of the major NAPs and helps to reduce congestion on the Internet.

Devices known as routers make sure that the packets of data sent from a computer on one ISP's network are sent to the intended machine on another local or wide-area network via the quickest, most efficient route, in accordance with communication protocols like TCP/IP. Just as the post office needs to know a street address before it can deliver a letter, routers need to know the address of the device to which information is being sent via the Internet. All devices communicating on the Internet, including servers used to host Web sites, have unique Internet Protocol (IP) addresses, which are four sets of numbers separated by decimals. Corresponding to numeric IP addresses are domain names, which are easier for humans to remember than long sequences of numbers. In the Web site address www.yahoo.com, .COM (like .ORG or .NET) is called the top-level domain and the word Yahoo is called the second-level domain. As the Internet evolved, a distributed database called the Domain Name System was created which contains all of the domain names and IP addresses associated with registered entities. Domain name servers located across the Internet are responsible for finding registered domain names and converting them to IP addresses so a connection can occur.

Institutions Overseeing Internet Infrastructure

In addition to the technical pieces of the Internet infrastructure, there are several organizations that regulate different aspects of it, or that seek to improve its stability and functionality. The Internet Society is a professional society that "provides leadership in addressing issues that confront the future of the Internet, and is the organization home for the groups responsible for Internet infrastructure standards, including the Internet Engineering Task Force (IETF) and the Internet Architecture Board (IAB)." The society's mission is "to assure the open development, evolution, and use of the Internet for the benefit of all people throughout the world."

According to the IAB, that organization is a technical advisory group whose responsibilities include providing "oversight of the architecture for the protocols and procedures used by the Internet." It "acts as a source of advice and guidance to the Board of Trustees and Officers of the Internet Society concerning technical, architectural, procedural, and (where appropriate) policy matters pertaining to the Internet and its enabling technologies." The IETF is "a large open international community of network designers, operators, vendors, and researchers concerned with the evolution of the Internet architecture and the smooth operation of the Internet."

Several other organizations were involved in overseeing the Internet in the early 2000s. The American Registry for Internet Numbers (ARIN) was a nonprofit organization that administered and registered IP numbers for North America, South America, the Caribbean, and sub-Saharan Africa. Two other regional Internet registries, Reseaux IP Europeens Network Coordination Centre (RIPE NCC), and the Asia Pacific Network Information Centre (APNIC) were responsible for administration and registration for the rest of the world.

The Internet Corporation for Assigned Names and Numbers (ICANN) was a non-profit corporation "formed to assume responsibility for the IP address space allocation, protocol parameter assignment, domain name system management, and root server system management functions previously performed under U.S. Government contract by IANA and other entities." Domain names were assigned to people or organizations through a registration process performed by a number of different registrars accredited by ICANN. A company called Network Solutions was responsible for keeping track of registered domain names to avoid duplication.

Finally, the World Wide Web Consortium was an organization responsible for developing "interoperable technologies (specifications, guidelines, software, and tools) to lead the Web to its full potential as a forum for information, commerce, communication, and collective understanding," and the Cooperative Association for Internet Data Analysis (CAIDA) collected, monitored, and analyzed information about Internet traffic patterns and performance that was useful to researchers, educators, and policy makers in a variety of fields.

Infrastructure Adequacy

By the early 2000s, the size of and traffic on the Internet had grown significantly. Research from Telcordia revealed that the number of Internet hosts, which includes things like routers, mail servers, workstations, and Web servers, increased 45 percent during 2000, reaching 100 million. At that time, the global population of Internet users was estimated to be 350 million. Furthermore, the kinds of services, including e-commerce, being performed on the Internet were growing in sophistication and complexity. Corresponding to this were increasing demands in the areas of network quality and performance.

Concerns existed regarding the ability of the Internet, and the communication protocols it relied on, to support the world's users. This was complicated by the Internet's large size and the fact that no one entity controlled it. Therefore, the quality, integrity, and performance of different areas of the network varied, and control was distributed to many different entities throughout the world.

One infrastructure concern that existed in the early 2000s concerned the ability of routers to handle the skyrocketing number of entries to the Internet backbone's routing table, which stores information about all of the existing network destinations on the Internet. This was leading to instability in the Internet's backbone routing infrastructure. Part of the problem involved large companies that engaged in multi-homing, a practice of connecting to two ISPs at once in case service with one failed. Although this helped to ensure a more consistent Internet connection (which is critical for e-commerce companies), the practice required a separate listing in the routing table for each ISP used.

Another concern involved the burgeoning number of international users in developing nations without the sophisticated infrastructure found in Europe and the United States. In March of 2001, Information-Week reported that although 100 million computers were connected to the Internet, that figure represented less than two percent of the world's population. It also explained that 88 percent of Internet users lived in industrialized nations.

This placed increased demands on limited resources in developing nations. Telecordia's research found that while the ratio of Internet users to hosts was 2.4 to one in the United States, the number was as high as 100 to one in countries like India where, according to eMarketer, less than one percent of the adult population has Internet access. In India, 2.2 phone lines exist per 100 people, and many of those are substandard for connecting to the Internet at appropriate speeds. Inadequate infrastructures in areas like India and Latin America have strong implications for e-commerce. Forrester Research predicted that by 2004, 85 percent of online trade will occur in only 12 countries, led by the United States and Western Europe. Although wireless and satellite connections were one solution for nations where ground-based network infrastructures were virtually non-existent, the Internet's TCP/IP protocol didn't work consistently well via satellite, requiring special software to remedy the problem.

Internet Backbone

In computer networking, a backbone is a central conduit designed to transfer network traffic at high speeds. Backbones connect local area networks (LANs) and wide area networks (WANs) together. Network backbones are designed to maximize the reliability and performance of large-scale, long-distance data communications. The best-known network backbones are those used on the Internet.

Internet Backbone Technology

Nearly all Web browsing, video streaming, and other common online traffic flows through Internet backbones. They consist of network routers and switches connected mainly by fiber optic cables (although some Ethernet segments on lower traffic backbone links also exist). Each fiber link on the backbone normally provides 100 Gbps of network bandwidth. Computers rarely connect to a backbone directly. Instead, the networks of Internet service providers or large organizations connect to these backbones and computers access the backbone indirectly.

In 1986, the U.S. National Science Foundation (NSF) established the first backbone network for the Internet. The first NSFNET link only provided 56 Kbps - performance laughable by today's standards - although it was quickly upgraded to a 1.544 MbpsT1 line and to 45 Mbps T3 by 1991. Many academic institutions and research organizations used NSFNET,

During the 1990s, the explosive growth of the Internet was largely funded by private companies who built their own backbones. The Internet eventually became a network of smaller backbones operated by Internet Service Providers that tap into the biggest national and internal backbones owned by large telecommunications companies.

Backbones and Link Aggregation

One technique for managing the very high volumes of data traffic that flow through network backbones is called link aggregation or trunking. Link aggregation involves the coordinated use of multiple physical ports on routers or switches for delivering a single stream of data. For example, four standard 100 Gbps links that would ordinarily support different data streams can be aggregated together to provide one, 400 Gbps conduit. Network administrators configure the hardware on each of the ends of the connection to support this trunking.

Issues with Network Backbones

Due to their central role on the Internet and global communications, backbone installations are a prime target for malicious attacks. Providers tend to keep the locations and some technical details of their backbones secret for this reason. One university study on Internet backbone conduits in the U.S., for example, required four years of research and still is incomplete.

National governments sometimes maintain tight control over their country's outbound backbone connections and can either censor or completely shut off Internet access to its citizens. The interactions between large corporations and their agreements for sharing each other's networks also tend to complex business dynamics. The concept of net neutrality relies on the owners and maintainers of backbone networks to observe national and international laws and conduct business fairly.

References

- Definition-of-backbone-817777: lifewire.com, Retrieved 29 May 2018

- Internet: searchwindevelopment.techtarget.com, Retrieved 25 April 2018

- Internet-access-7776: techopedia.com, Retrieved 15 June 2018

- Connect-methods: steves-internet-guide.com, Retrieved 19 July 2018

- Internet-infrastructure, encyclopedias-almanacs-transcripts-and-maps: encyclopedia.com, Retrieved 29 June 2018

## 2

Networks: An Introduction

A computer or data network is a system of digital telecommunication, which facilitates the exchange of resources across nodes. The topics elucidated in this chapter provide an insight into this field through the elucidation of the varied types of computer networks such as LAN, WAN, PAN, WLAN, etc.

In information technology, a computer network, also called a data network, is a series of points, or nodes, interconnected by communication paths for the purpose of transmitting, receiving and exchanging data, voice and video traffic.

Network devices including switches and routers use a variety of protocols and algorithms to exchange information and to transport data to its intended endpoint. Every endpoint (sometimes called a host) in a network has a unique identifier, often an IP address or a Media Access Control address, that is used to indicate the source or destination of the transmission. Endpoints can include servers, personal computers, phones and many types of network hardware.

Wired and Wireless Technologies

Networks may use a mix of wired and wireless technologies. Network devices communicate through a wired or wireless transmission medium. In wired networks, this may consist of optical fiber, coaxial cable or copper wires in the form of a twisted pair. Wireless network pathways include computer networks that use wireless data connections for connecting endpoints. These endpoints include broadcast radio, cellular radio, microwave and satellite.

Networks can be private or public. Private networks require the user to obtain permission to gain access. Typically, this is granted either manually by a network administrator or obtained directly by the user via a password or with other credentials. Public networks like the internet do not restrict access.

LANs, WANs, MANs and SANs

Networks may also be categorized by the scope of their domains. Local area networks (LANs) interconnect endpoints in a single domain. Wide area networks interconnect multiple LANs, and metropolitan area networks interconnect computer resources in a geographic area. Storage area networks interconnect storage devices and resources. Networks may also be divided into sub networks, also called subnets.

Network protocols and standards specify exactly how data should be transmitted and received. Modern, packet switched networks use protocols -- TCP/IP being the most widespread -- to establish a standard means of communication. The Ethernet standard establishes a common language for wired networks to communicate; the 802.11 standard does the same for wireless LANs.

A network's capacity -- that is, how much traffic it can transmit at any one time -- is measured in terms of bandwidth. Bandwidth is quantified by the theoretical maximum number of bits per second that can pass through a network device. Throughput is a measure of the actual speed of a successful transmission after accounting for factors like latency, processing power and protocol overhead.

Characteristics of a Computer Network

- Share resources from one computer to another.

- Create files and store them in one computer, access those files from the other computer(s) connected over the network.

- Connect a printer, scanner, or a fax machine to one computer within the network and let other computers of the network use the machines available over the network.

Following is the list of hardware's required to set up a computer network:

- Network Cables
- Distributors
- Routers
- Internal Network Cards
- External Network Cards

Types of Computer Network Topologies

Network topologies represent the physical or logical structure of a network, with common topologies that include the following major types:

- Full mesh networks, in which all nodes are connected to each other and can exchange data.

- Partial mesh networks, in which some of the nodes are connected to each other in a full mesh scheme, but others are only connected to one or two other nodes in the network.

- Point to point networks, which is a connection between only two end points.

- Network fabric, in which endpoints transfer data to each other through interconnecting switches and can connect to any other by taking a path through a crisscross pattern of connections.

- A tree network, which is a combination of two or more star networks connected together.

- A star network, in which the nodes are connected to a common central computer.

- A Bus, a circuit arrangement where all network devices are attached directly to a transmission line directly, and while all signals pass through all devices, each device has a unique identity and recognizes signals intended for it.

Network Topologies and Types of Networks

The term network topology describes the relationship of connected devices in terms of a geometric graph. Devices are represented as vertices, and their connections are represented as edges on the graph. It describes how many connections each device has, in what order, and it what sort of hierarchy.

Typical network configurations include the bus topology, mesh topology, ring topology, star topology, tree topology and hybrid topology.

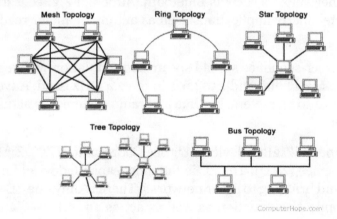

Most home networks are configured in a tree topology that is connected to the Internet. Corporate networks often use tree topologies, but they typically incorporate star topologies and an Intranet.

Personal Area Network

A personal area network, or PAN, is a computer network that enables communication between computer devices near a person. PANs can be wired, such as USB or FireWire, or they can be wireless, such as infrared, ZigBee, Bluetooth and ultrawideband, or UWB. The range of a PAN typically is a few meters. Examples of wireless PAN, or WPAN, devices include cell phone headsets, wireless keyboards, wireless mice, printers, bar code scanners and game consoles.

Wireless PANs feature battery-operated devices that draw very little current. Sleep modes commonly are used to further extend battery life. Network protocols tend be simpler than Wi-Fi or WiMAX (to reduce required processor power), and the transmit power is typically less than 1 mill watt.

In the United States, PANs for the most part operate in two unlicensed bands: 902-928 MHz and 2.4-2.4835 GHz. Ultra wideband devices also can operate in the 3.1-10.6 GHz band, coexisting with other radio services by employing low overall power and ultra-low power densities (watts/Hz).

Let's examine three of the most popular PAN technologies: ZigBee, Bluetooth and ultra wideband.

ZigBee is a short-range, low-power computer networking protocol that complies with the IEEE 802.15.4 standard. In the U.S., ZigBee devices operate in the 902-928 MHz and 2.4 GHz unlicensed bands. The technology is intended to be less complex and less expensive than other WPANs such as Bluetooth. Although ZigBee is a WPAN protocol, it also is used for telemetry applications such as automatic meter reading and building automation.

ZigBee employs direct-sequence spread spectrum modulation with a gross data rate of 40 kb/s in the 900 MHz band and 250 kb/s in the 2.4 GHz band. Advertised transmission range is from 10 to 75 meters, but like any radio system, the actual range depends on the environment.

There are three types of ZigBee devices: ZigBee Coordinator (ZC), ZigBee Router (ZR), and ZigBee End Device (ZED). The ZC is the most capable device, forming the root of the network tree and bridging to other networks. There is only one ZC per network. The ZR can run an application function as well as act as an intermediate router, passing data from other devices. A ZED contains just enough functionality to talk to its parent node, which is a coordinator or a router. It can sleep most of the time, extending its battery life.

The ZigBee Alliance is a trade organization charged with developing and publishing the Zigbee standard and promoting its use.

Bluetooth is a computer networking protocol designed for short-range, low-power communications in the 2.4 GHz unlicensed band. It was named after King Harald Bluetooth, ruler of Denmark and Norway in the late 10th century. Sven Mattison and Jaap Haartsen, both employees of Ericsson Mobile Platforms in Lund, Sweden, published the first Bluetooth standard in 1994. The current version of the standard is 2.1 and specifies gross data rates up to 3 Mb/s.

Bluetooth employs frequency-hopping spread spectrum modulation with a rate of up to 1600 hops per second using 79 different channels, each 1 MHz wide. Because the technology uses a spread spectrum signal and low power, it is less likely to cause harmful interference to other 2.4 GHz devices, such as Wi-Fi radios, that often exist in the same personal computer. There are three classes of Bluetooth devices corresponding to different transmit power levels. Class 1, 2 and 3 devices operate at up to 100 mW, 2.5 mW and 1 mW, respectively.

Bluetooth networks normally operate in a master-slave configuration. A master device can communicate with up to seven active slave devices, and this network of up to eight devices is called a piconet. Up to 255 additional devices can be inactive or parked, waiting for wakeup instructions from the master.

The technology implements confidentiality, authentication and key derivation using algorithms based on the SAFER+ block cipher.

The Bluetooth Special Interest Group is a privately held, nonprofit trade association organized to promote Bluetooth in the marketplace and to develop Bluetooth standards.

Ultrawideband is a radio technology useful for short-range, high-bandwidth communications that does not create harmful interference to users sharing the same band. By FCC definition, a UWB signal has a bandwidth that exceeds the lesser of 500 MHz or 20% of the arithmetic center frequency. Such a bandwidth exceeds all conventional spread spectrum radio systems, and the resulting low power density ensures the signal does not cause harmful interference.

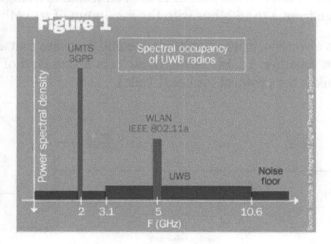

The FCC allows UWB devices to operate in the 3.1-10.6 GHz band. In this band, the emission limit is -41.3 dBm per MHz, which is the Part 15 limit for unintentional emissions in this band. Unlike conventional radios, which continuously modulate a sinusoidal carrier, UWB radios are short-duration pulse generators. The occupied bandwidth is roughly equal to the inverse of the pulse duration. The duty cycle of UWB signals is usually quite low, but the net throughput is still high because the burst information rate during the pulse can be more than 100 Mb/s.

A pulse-based UWB method is the basis of the IEEE 802.15.4a draft standard and working group, which has proposed UWB as an alternative physical layer protocol to ZigBee.

The WiMedia Alliance is a trade association organized to promote UWB and develop standards.

In addition to these three, other WPANs include Wibree, an ultra-low-power complement to Bluetooth; Wireless USB; EnOcean, composed of self-powered devices; and 6loWPAN, which allows IPv6 packets to ride 802.15.4 networks.

Local Area Network

The local area network (LAN) is a network which is designed to operate over a small physical area such as an office, factory or a group of buildings. LANs are very widely used in a variety of applications.

The personal computers and workstations in the offices are interconnected via LAN to share resources. The resources to be shared can be hardware like a printer or softwares or data. A LAN is a form of local (limited-distance), shared packet network for computer communications. In LAN all the machines are connected to a single cable. The data rates for LAN range from 4 to 16 Mbps with the maximum of 100 Mbps.

The term LAN can also refer just to the hardware and software that allows you to connect all the devices together. In this sense, Local Talk is one kind of LAN, Ethernet is another. (AppleTalk is the protocol for Local Talk.)

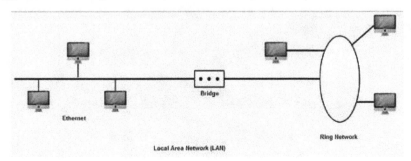

Local Area Network (LAN)

The components used by LANs can be divided into cabling standards, hardware, and protocols. Various LAN protocols are Ethernet, Token Ring: TCP/IP, 5MB, NetBIOS and NetBeui, IPX/SPX, Fiber Distributed Data Interchange (FDDI) and Asynchronous Transfer Mode (ATM).

Types of LAN

Ethernet is the most common type of LAN. Different Lan can be differentiated on the behalf of following characteristics.

Topology: The topology is the geometric arrangement of a network elements. For example, Network devices can be interconnected in a ring topology or in a bus topology or linear bus.

Protocols: It is a guidelines for communicating data between two devices. The protocols also determine type of error and data compression.

Media: The cable used in Lan to connect devices are twisted-pair wire, coaxial cables, or fiber optic.

Example of Lan Topologies

Various topologies are possible for the broadcast LANs such as bus topology or ring topology.

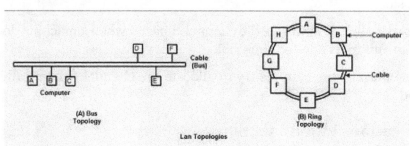

Lan Topologies

1. Bus Topology

- Bus topology is shown in Fig. In this topology at any instant only one computer acts as master and it is allowed to transmit (broadcast). The others are supposed to listen.

- If two or more machines want to transmit simultaneously then an arbitration mechanism has to be used for resolving the conflict.

- It is possible to have a centralized or distributed type arbitration mechanism.

- The most popular example of bus topology is Ethernet (IEEE 802.3). It has a decentralized control and it operates at 10 or 100 Mbps.

- Computers on Ethernet can transmit whenever they want. If collision of their packets takes place, then they wait for a random time and retransmit their packets.

2. Ring Topology

- This is another broadcast topology.

- In a ring each bit propagates around on its own without waiting for the rest of the packet to which it belongs.

- Since it is a broadcast system, some rules are essential for arbitrating the simultaneous access to the ring.

- An example of ring based LAN is IEEE 802.5 (IBM token ring) operating at 4 and 16 Mbps.

Static and Dynamic Broadcast Networks

- The broadcast networks are further classified into two types namely:

  1. Static networks and

  2. Dynamic networks.

- This classification is based on how the channel is allocated.

- In static allocation, each machine is allowed to broadcast only in its allotted time slot.

- But static allocation wastes the channel capacity when a machine does not want to transmit in its allotted time slot.

- Hence most of the systems try to allocate the channel dynamically i.e. on demand.

LAN Applications and Benefits

LANs are used almost exclusively for data communications over relatively short distances such as within an office, office building or campus environment. LANs allow multiple workstations to share access to multiple host computers, other workstations, printers and other peripherals, and connections to other networks. LANs are also being utilized for imaging applications, as well. They are also being used for video and voice communications, although currently on a very limited basis.

LAN applications include communications between the workstation and host computers, other workstations, and servers. The servers may allow sharing of resources. Resources could be information, data files, e-mail, voice mail, software, hardware (hard disk, printer, fax, etc.) and other networks.

LAN benefits include the fact that a high-speed transmission system can be shared among multiple devices in support of large number of active terminals and a large number of active applications in the form of a multi-user, multi-tasking computer network.

LAN-connected workstations realize the benefit of decentralized access to very substantial centralized processors, perhaps in the form of mainframe host computer and storage capabilities (information repositories). Additionally, current technology allows multiple LANs to be inter-networked through the use of LAN switches, routers and the like.

Wireless Local Area Network

Wireless local area network solutions comprise one of the fastest growing segments of the telecommunications industry. The finalization of industry standards, and the corresponding release of WLAN products by leading manufacturers, has sparked the implementation of WLAN solutions in many market segments, including small office/home office (SOHO), large corporations, manufacturing plants, and public hotspots such as airports, convention centers, hotels, and even coffee shops.

In some instances WLAN technology is used to save costs and avoid laying cable, while in other cases it is the only option for providing high-speed Internet access to the public. Whatever the reason, WLAN solutions are popping up everywhere.

To address this growing demand, traditional networking companies, as well as new players to the market, have released a variety of WLAN products. These products typically implement one of the many WLAN standards, although dual-mode products that support multiple standards are starting to emerge as well. When evaluating these products, some key areas should be considered, including:

- Range/coverage. The range for WLAN products is anywhere from 50 meters to 150 meters.

- Throughput. The data transfer rate ranges from 1 Mbps to 54 Mbps.

- Interference. Some standards will experience interference from standard household electronics and other wireless networking technologies.

- Power consumption. The amount of power consumed by the wireless adapter differs between product offerings, often depending on standards they implement.

- Cost. The cost of a solution can vary significantly depending on the requirements of the deployment and which standard is being implemented.

WLAN Configurations

Wireless LAN configurations range from extremely simple to very complex. The simplest WLAN is an independent, peer-to-peer configuration where two or more devices with wireless adapters connect to each other, as depicted in. Peer-to-peer configurations are often called ad hoc networks since they do not require any administration or preconfiguration. They also do not require the use of an access point, as each adapter communicates directly to another adapter without going through a central location.

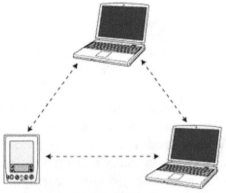

Peer-to-peer WLAN configuration.

Peer-to-peer networks are very useful when a group of users need to communicate with one another in an unstructured way. These networks can be extended by adding a wireless access point (AP) to the configuration. The AP can act as a repeater between the devices, essentially doubling the range of operation. In addition, access points can provide connectivity to a wired network allowing wireless users to share the wired network resources. illustrates this configuration.

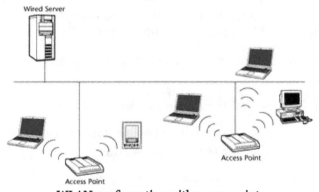

WLAN configuration with access point.

In a SOHO environment, access points can be used to provide multiple users access to a single high-speed connection without having to run Ethernet wires to each computer. In a corporate environment, many access points can work together to provide wireless coverage for an entire building or campus. The coverage area from each access point is called a microcell. To ensure coverage over a large area, the microcells will overlap at their boundaries, allowing users to freely move between cells without losing connectivity. This movement between a cluster of access points in a wireless network is called roaming. Roaming is made possible by a handoff mechanism whereby one access point passes the client information to another access point. This entire process is invisible to the client.

In more advanced configurations, extension points (EP) may be used in conjunction with access points. These EPs extend the range of the network by relaying signals to client devices, other EPs, or to an access point. They do not have to be tethered to the wired network, making it possible to service far-reaching clients. One other piece of WLAN equipment is a directional antenna. It allows a signal to be extended to locations many kilometers away. At the second location, the antenna is then connected to an access point, which provides wireless LAN connectivity for the rest of the facility.

WLAN Standards

Two standards bodies, IEEE and European Telecommunications Standards Institute (ETSI) and one technology alliance (HomeRF) promote WLAN standards. In the IEEE 802.11 family of WLANs, three standards deserve individual attention, and a handful of others are worth a quick mention. The leading standard is 802.11b, or Wi-Fi, short for Wireless Fidelity. The clear challenger is 802.11a, which provides increased throughput at a higher, less cluttered frequency; the outside contender is 802.11g, which just completed the final stage of IEEE approval at the time of writing. Other WLAN standards that are worth consideration are HIPERLAN/1 and HIPERLAN/2. We will provide information on each of these standards to give you a firm understanding of their technical and business advantages.

802.11

The IEEE 802.11 specification was approved in July 1997, making it the first wireless LAN standard to be defined. It uses the same switching protocols as wired Ethernet, but allows communication to happen without wires, instead using unlicensed 2.4-GHz frequency radio communication. Two frequency modulation techniques are supported in 802.11: FHSS and DSSS. 802.11 products are not commonly sold anymore, as updated versions (802.11a and 802.11b) have taken its place, providing higher bandwidths at a lower cost.

802.11b/Wi-Fi

802.11b is the most popular standard in the 802.11x family. The specification was approved at the same time as 802.11a in 1999, but since then has achieved broad market acceptance for wireless networking. 802.11b is based on the DSSS version of 802.11, using the 2.4-GHz spectrum. Since DSSS is easier to implement than orthogonal frequency division multiplexing (OFDM), as used in 802.11a, 802.11b products came to market much sooner than their 802.11a counterparts. In addition, the 2.4-GHz spectrum is available globally for WLAN configurations, while the 5-GHz spectrum that 802.11a uses is for limited uses in many countries.

802.11b is able to reach a maximum capacity of 11 Mbps. This surpassed the 10 Mbps speed that is part of the original Ethernet standard, making 802.11b a practical alternative to, or extension of, a wired LAN. To help foster interoperability between 802.11b products, the Wi-Fi Alliance [formerly the Wireless Ethernet Compatibility Alliance (WECA)] has set up certification the aforementioned Wireless Fidelity, or Wi-Fi. Obtaining Wi-Fi certification ensures that 802.11b products will be able to interoperate with other Wi-Fi products globally. This certification, combined with the release of 802.11b products by leading networking companies such as Cisco, Lucent, Agere Systems, Proxim, and 3Com, has made 802.11b the leading WLAN standard.

The use of the 2.4-GHz band for communication has advantages and disadvantages. On the plus side, the 2.4-GHz spectrum is almost universally available for WLAN configurations. Initially, a few countries did not allow for its usage, but this has changed thanks to lobbying by industry groups. Additionally, 2.4-GHz signals are able to penetrate physical barriers such as walls and ceilings more effectively than higher frequencies can. The downside of using the 2.4-GHz spectrum is congestion. Since it is unlicensed, meaning anyone can use it without obtaining a special license, other electronic products also use this frequency for communication. Two common examples are cordless phones and microwave ovens. With the widespread use of this spectrum, there is a possibility that it will become overcrowded, resulting in too much interference for effective data communication. Hopefully, this will not be the case since any manufacturer of any product that uses the 2.4-GHz band is required to take interference into account in its product design.

One interesting point about the 802.11b specification is how it handles roaming between access points. The specification requires a method for roaming, but leaves the implementation up to the AP manufacturer. This will make roaming between different vendors' access points difficult, as it is unlikely that manufacturers will employ the same handoff routines.

In typical indoor office configurations, an 802.11b access point can communicate with devices up to 100 meters (around 300 feet) away. The further away a terminal is from the access point, the slower the communication will be. Devices within about 30 meters can usually achieve a raw data transfer rate of 11 Mbps; beyond 30 meters, the rate drops to 5.5 Mbps, and then to 2 Mbps around 65 meters away, and finally, to 1 Mbps around the outer edge. These numbers represent the anticipated coverage area and transmission speeds, but the products from each vendor will differ in performance. If you are looking to implement an 802.11b WLAN, it is recommended that you do a site survey to obtain the actual operating range and associated bandwidth for your location.

802.11b Security

When the IEEE created the 802.11 specification, it implemented a feature called Wired Equivalent Privacy (WEP) with the intent of providing basic levels of authentication and data encryption. As the name suggests, the goal of WEP is to provide an equivalent level of security as normally present in an unsecured wired LAN. This is clearly important, as wireless networks do not have the physical protection that wired environments do. Both 802.11a and 802.11b specifications use WEP.

For authentication, an access point that has WEP enabled will send a text request to the client to verify the client's identity. The client uses RC4 encryption with a secret key to encrypt the text, then returns the encrypted text back to the access point. Once received, the access point decrypts the text using the same key. If the text matches the text that was sent, then the client is authenticated and granted access. For encryption, WEP provides a 24-bit initialization vector that augments the WEP key. This vector changes with each packet, thereby providing a basic level of data encryption.

Unfortunately, both forms of WEP security present some concerns. For authentication, WEP supports no more than four keys and provides no mechanism for refreshing those keys on a regular basis. The result is that the same keys are used by multiple clients and access points and are never changed. This means that malicious users can "listen" to the communication stream and, by using freely available software, very quickly authenticate themselves to the access point. For the encryption layer, WEP uses RC4 in what is called a one-time-pad manner. The security of a one-time-pad is only as secure as the pad being used, which for WEP is the 24 bits. This means that the onetime-pad is repeated at least every 224 packets. For access points with moderate amounts of traffic, this is a matter of hours, hence, attackers monitoring the data stream could detect two messages encrypted with the same 24-bit initialization vector and be able to determine the keys and decipher the plain text.

Companies should realize that WEP was never designed to provide end-to-end security. It is intended for usage in conjunction with existing security mechanisms such as firewalls, virtual private networks (VPNs), and application-level security. The following are some suggestions for corporations that are using, or planning on using, WEP security as part of their WLAN:

- Use a firewall to separate the wireless network from the wired network.
- Have the wireless users authenticate with a VPN to access the corporate network.
- Incorporate security at the application level for highly confidential information.
- Implement dynamic key refreshing for the WEP keys.
- Do not assume that WEP guarantees absolute data privacy.

Not all of the 802.11 WLAN security issues can be attributed to problems with WEP. Many of these issues have resulted from companies not using the WEP for its original purpose or from not using it at all. By implementing additional security mechanisms as listed, corporations can ensure secure wireless communication. In addition, the 802.11i Task Group is working additional levels of security for 802.11 WLANs. The first component of the 802.11i draft is currently being implemented in the form of Wi-Fi Protected Access. Wi-Fi Protected Access offers increased security over WEP.

802.11a

802.11a is a high-speed alternative to 802.11b, transmitting at 5 GHz and speeds up to 54 Mbps. Unlike 802.11 and 802.11b, 802.11a uses OFDM modulation technology. This, along with the difference in frequency, makes 802.11a networks incompatible with 802.11b networks. Due to the increased complexity of 802.11a, the first products did not reach the market until early 2002, with all the chipsets being provided by a single vendor, Atheros Communications. Since then other vendors have released 802.11a chipsets, helping 802.11a gain broader market acceptance and interoperability certification.

The Wi-Fi Alliance has included certification for 802.11a products within the Wi-Fi certification program. They are using the same name for both 802.11b and 802.11a to help reduce confusion in the market and to foster growth of the emerging 802.11a products. The Wi-Fi Alliance are hoping that Wi-Fi certification will have the same effect on the 802.11a market as it did on the 802.11b market. Certification gives consumers confidence that the products they are purchasing will work with other products based on the same specification.

The move to the 5-GHz band and OFDM modulation provides two important benefits over 802.11b. First, it increases the maximum speed per channel from 11 Mbps to 54 Mbps. This is a tremendous boost, especially considering that the bandwidth is shared among all the users on an access point. The increased speed is especially useful for wireless multimedia, large file transfers, and fast Internet access. Second, the bandwidth available in the 5-GHz range is larger than available at 2.4 GHz, allowing for more simultaneous users without potential conflicts. Additionally, the 5-GHz band is not as congested at the 2.4-GHz band, resulting in less interference.

These advantages come with some downsides. The higher operating frequency equates to a shorter range. This means that to maintain the high data rates, a larger number of 802.11a access points are required to cover the same area, versus 802.11b. While 802.11b access points have a typical range of 100 meters, 802.11a access points are often limited to between 25 and 50 meters. In addition, OFDM requires more power than DSSS, leading to higher power consumption by 802.11a products. This is definitely a disadvantage for mobile devices that have limited battery power. Another downside is that 802.11a and 802.11b products are not compatible. With the large number of 802.11b products on the market, this will have a negative effect on the adoption of 802.11a products. That said, both standards can coexist, and products are now on the market that support both 802.11a and 802.11b in a single chipset. This dual-mode approach is very attractive for users who want the advantages of 802.11a, with the backward compatibility and market penetration of 802.11b.

One final item to note about 802.11a is that the 5-GHz frequency is not universally available for WLAN products. Many European countries, as well as Japan, are resisting the adoption of 802.11a as a standard, leaving some doubt as to whether it will become a global standard as 802.11b has.

802.11g

IEEE 802.11g brings high-speed wireless communication to the 2.4-GHz band, while maintaining backward compatibility with 802.11b. This is accomplished on two layers. First, 802.11g operate on the same 2.4-GHz frequency band as 802.11b, with the same DSSS modulation types for speeds up to 11 Mbps. For 54 Mbps, 802.11g use the more efficient OFDM modulation types, still within the 2.4-GHz band. In practice, an 802.11g network card will be able to work with an 802.11b access point, and 802.11b cards will work with an 802.11g access point. In both of these scenarios, the 802.11b component is the limiting factor, so the maximum speed is 11 Mbps. To obtain the 54-Mbps speeds, both the network cards and access point have to be 802.11g compliant. In all other aspects, such as network capacity and range, 802.11b and 802.11g are the same.

Since 802.11g offers the same speed as 802.11a, comparisons between them are inevitable. And because they both use OFDM modulation, the main differences result from their frequency ranges and corresponding bandwidth. The total available bandwidth at 2.4 GHz remains the same as with 802.11b. This results in lower capacity for 802.11g WLANs when compared to 802.11a. In addition, fewer channels are available, leading to a higher potential of conflicts. When we take into consideration the backward compatibility that 802.11g has with 802.11b, 802.11g becomes an attractive option for companies that have 802.11b installations.

Other 802.11 Standards

Just as 802.11g improved upon 802.11b, other 802.11 task groups are in place to improve upon the exiting 802.11x standards. The areas of concentration are security, quality of service, compliance, and interoperability. All of these are still in the task group stage of the specification process:

- IEEE 802.11e. Aimed at providing quality of service (QoS) capabilities to enable reliable voice communication to complement 802.11b systems. 802.11e will also provide enhanced security and authentication mechanisms. It is expected to receive final IEEE approval in 2003.

- IEEE 802.11f. Aimed at developing the recommended practices for an Inter-Access Point Protocol (IAPP) to achieve multivendor access point interoperability.

- IEEE 802.11h. Aimed at enhancing the 802.11a High-Speed Physical layer in the 5-GHz band to make IEED 802.11a products compliant with European regulatory requirements.

- IEEE 802.11i. Aimed at enhancing the 802.11 MAC layer to increase security and authentication mechanisms.

HomeRF

As the name suggests, HomeRF is a wireless LAN technology aimed at home wireless networking. It is based on the 802.11 FHSS standard, but enhancements have been made to meet the unique needs of the average consumer. HomeRF uses the Shared Wireless Access Protocol (SWAP). One of the major enhancements of SWAP is its support for high-quality voice communication. Additionally, the HomeRF specification incorporates the Digital Enhanced Cordless Telephony (DECT) standard. This allows cordless phones to use the same home networking infrastructure as PCs and appliances while providing advanced telephony features, including call waiting, caller ID, call forwarding, and personal ringtones.

The HomeRF specification has been designed for ease of use and price rather than bandwidth and performance. HomeRF networks provide a range of up to 50 meters (around 150 feet) with maximum speeds at 10 Mbps. The first generation of HomeRF products provided throughput of 1.6 Mbps. HomeRF uses the 2.4-GHz frequency band so it will experience similar interference as 802.11b from household appliances such as microwaves.

With wide industry adoption of 802.11b, HomeRF products have not been able to reach critical mass. The major advantages of HomeRF over 802.11b are ease of use, cost, and telephony support, all areas being addressed by 802.11b products and upcoming 802.11x specifications. For this reason among others, the HomeRF Consortium disbanded in early 2003, making HomeRF a defunct standard.

HIPERLAN/1 and HIPERLAN/2

The European Telecommunications Standards Institute (ETSI) proposed the High-Performance Radio Local Area Network (HIPERLAN) standard in 1992 to address the need for high-speed short-range wireless communication. This first version is commonly referred to as HIPERLAN/1. It is based on Ethernet standards, with its radio transmission taken from GSM. It uses the 5-GHz frequency band. The operating range and bandwidth is difficult to determine since HIPERLAN/1 did not experience commercial success. According to the specification, HIPERLAN/1 has data rates approaching 23.5 Mbps.

HIPERLAN/2 is the next-generation WLAN specification from ETSI Broadband Radio Access Networks (BRAN). It continues to use the 5-GHz frequency band, but with OFDM technology. It is able to achieve peak speeds of 54 Mbps with an approximate range of 150 meters (450 feet).

HIPERLAN/2 has been designed to address the various market segments where WLANs are used: enterprise networking, SOHO, and 3G wireless hotspots. To this end, it has incorporated QoS for real-time multimedia communication, efficient power consumption for portable devices, strong security and interoperability with Ethernet, IEEE 1394 (Firewire), and 3G mobile systems. The specification also permits roaming between HIPERLAN/2 access points, making it suitable for corporate environments. As of late 2002, HIPERLAN/2 still has not seen any meaningful adoption in either the consumer or corporate space.

Campus Area Network

A campus area network known as (CAN) is used to inter-connect networks in limited geographical locality like university campus, military bases, or organizational campuses etc. It can be taken as the metropolitan network that has the specific settings at the small area just like a computer lab in the university.

CAN (Campus Area Network) area is no doubt larger than a local area network but it is still smaller then a wide area network. These networks are designed for the particular place that hits the highest point level. For example, multiple labs, multiple offices in the buildings etc. most of the time, this term is referred as the university campus but when it is used at organizational level, we call it corporate campus network.

It is smaller than a wide area network and multiple Local Area Network (LAN) combines in one organization or regions to make a Campus Area Network (CAN). Therefore, whenever some one tells you about the networks within the specific area, you can easily guess that it is campus network.

Infrastructure of CAN (Campus Area Network)

In this kind of networking, the same technology along with the hardware is used in different buildings of one campus or one corporation. They follow the same terminologies like the local area networks but the difference is that they are interconnected between the multiple buildings at the particular location. Just imagine a university campus in which you have multiple departments such as information technology, electronics, mass communication and fine arts etc. and in all these departments computer labs, they have implemented the same infra -structure of hardware and other technologies using the Local area network as the main tool, and one message sent by one department can be accessed by the other department, then we say that the network is following the techniques of Campus Area Network (CAN).

Same is the case with the corporation or organizations which have different departments in one locality and these departments can communicate with each other using the communication medium of CAN (Campus Area Network). In Campus Area Networking (CAN) system the same type of hardware means that routers, switches, hubs, cabling and even wireless connection points are same in the multiple buildings. We can say that theses all networking resources are owned by the same organization. If we talk about the internet connection companies, we see that one university uses the same connection for all of its departments. In CAN (Campus Area Network), just like the internet connection, one company has dealings with the entire organization.

How CAN (Campus Area Networks) Work, Uses of CAN As we know that universities are the best example of this type of interconnection hence, different blocks of universities such as administrative office, educational departments, staff rooms, gymnasium, common room, hostels and conference halls when connected with each other combine to form the CAN (Campus Area Network). In most cases, corporate campuses are connected through the wireless communication mediums rather than cabling and wirings because they are more economical to use as compare to the long wiring and cabling. Organizations do follow this strategy because they always try to maintain the best outcome by investing less and with the wireless communication throughout their building offices, they can manage their budget that they may be spending on the wiring, hubs, switches etc. they can perform the same task by only connecting one or two devices at their main office and providing signals to other departments which they can use without any difficulty.

Campus Area networks (CAN) are economical, beneficial and easy to implement in the specific kilometers of locality. It is very helpful for the universities and other corporate organizations to work from any block and receive the same speed of data transfer.

Metropolitan Area Network

A large computer network which extends to a city or to a large university campus is termed as metropolitan area network or MAN. The purpose of MAN (Metropolitan Area Network) is to provide the link to the internet in the long run. A MAN (Metropolitan Area Network) usually incorporates a number of LANs to form a network. This large network MANs (Metropolitan Area Network) backbone comprises of an optical fiber set-up.

Types of MAN (metropolitan Area Network) Technologies

Most widely used technologies to develop a MAN (Metropolitan Area Network) network are FDDI (fiber distribution data interface), ATM (Asynchronous Transfer Mode) and SMDS (switched multi megabit data service). ATM (Asynchronous Transfer Mode) is the most frequently used of all. ATM (Asynchronous Transfer Mode) is a digital data transfer technology. It was developed in 1980 to improve the transportation of real time data over a single network. ATM (Asynchronous Transfer Mode) works just like cell relay system, where data is separated in the form of fixed equal sized packets and is transferred overtime. The purpose of ATM (Asynchronous Transfer Mode) was to access clear audio and video results during a video conferencing. The attributes of ATM has enabled it to become a base of wide area data networking.

ATM (Asynchronous Transfer Mode) combines the characteristics of circuit switching and packet switching, which allows it to transfer even the real time data. FDDI is a standard for data transfer over LAN, which can be extended to the range of approximately 200kms. FDDI can help support the data transmission of many thousand users. This is the reason why it is referred to as the MAN (Metropolitan Area Network) technology. FDDI uses optical fiber for its basic infrastructure that is why it is referred to as fiber distribution data interface. When data is transferred through a connectionless service we use the technology named as SMDS. Connectionless service implies that data is transferred by storing the information in the header and it reaches its destination independently through any network. When the data is transferred using the technology of SMDS, it also forms small data packets just like in ATM. However SMDS allows the transmission of data over large geographical areas in the form of datagrams (the data packets of an unreliable data service provider). Nowadays MAN (Metropolitan Area Network) links are established using infrared and microwave signals.

Functioning of Metropolitan Area Networks (MAN)

MAN (Metropolitan Area Network) usually falls between LAN and WAN. It is generally applied to connect geographically dispersed LANs. Therefore the goal of MAN is to develop a communication link between two independent LAN nodes. A MAN (Metropolitan Area Network) is usually established using optical fiber. The network is established using routers and switches. A switch is a port which is active in handling the filtration of data usually coming in the form of frames. Any switch acts as a dual port, at one end it is handling filtration of data and at the other end managing connections. Router is another device for facilitating the network connection. Router helps the data packets to identify the path to be taken. Hence in other words it keeps an eye on the data transfer. MAN (Metropolitan Area Network) is usually operated over an area of up to 50kms.

Advantages of MAN (Metropolitan Area Network)

MAN (Metropolitan Area Network) falls in between the LAN and WAN. It therefore increases the efficiency of handling data while at the same time saves the cost attached to establish a wide area network. MAN (Metropolitan Area Network) offers centralized management of data. It enables you to connect many fast LANs together. Telephone companies worldwide have facilitated the transfer of data with the help of an under-ground optical fiber network. These optical fibers increase the efficiency and speed of data transfer. The optical fibers enable you to access a speed of almost 1000mbps. If you develop a WAN of 1.45 mbps its cost is more than what it gives you. Whereas when you establish metropolitan area network it offers you the speed of 1000mbps as a whole with the lowest cost involved.

Wide Area Network (WAN)

A WAN (wide area network) is a communications network that spans a large geograph-ic area such as across cities, states, or countries. They can be private to connect parts of a business or they can be more public to connect smaller networks together.

The easiest way to understand what a WAN is to think of the internet as a whole, which is the world's largest WAN. The internet is a WAN because, through the use of ISPs, it connects lots of smaller local area networks (LANs) or metro area networks (MANs).

On a smaller scale, a business may have a WAN that's comprised of cloud services, its headquarters, and smaller branch offices. The WAN, in this case, would be used to con-nect all of those sections of the business together.

No matter what the WAN joins together or how far apart the networks are, the end re-sult is always intended to allow different smaller networks from different locations to communicate with one another.

How WANs are Connected

Since WANs, by definition, cover a larger distance than LANs, it makes sense to con-nect the various parts of the WAN using a virtual private network (VPN). This provides protected communications between sites, which is necessary given that the data trans-fers are happening over the internet.

Although VPNs provide reasonable levels of security for business uses, a public inter-net connection does not always provide the predictable levels of performance that a dedicated WAN link can. This is why fiber optic cables are sometimes used to facilitate communication between the WAN links.

X.25, Frame Relay, and MPLS

Since the 1970s, many WANs were built using a technology standard called X.25. These types of networks supported automated teller machines, credit card transaction sys-tems, and some of the early online information services such as CompuServe. Older X.25 networks ran using 56 Kbps dial-up modem connections.

Frame Relay technology was created to simplify X.25 protocols and provide a less ex-pensive solution for wide area networks that needed to run at higher speeds. Frame

Relay became a popular choice for telecommunications companies in the United States during the 1990s, particularly AT&T.

Multiprotocol Label Switching (MPLS) was built to replace Frame Relay by improving protocol support for handling voice and video traffic in addition to normal data traffic. The Quality of Service (QoS) features of MPLS was key to its success. So-called "triple play" network services built on MPLS increased in popularity during the 2000s and eventually replaced Frame Relay.

Leased Lines and Metro Ethernet

Many businesses started using leased line WANs in the mid-1990s as the web and internet exploded in popularity. T1 and T3 lines are often used to support MPLS or internet VPN communications.

Long-distance, point-to-point Ethernet links can also be used to build dedicated wide area networks. While much more expensive than internet VPNs or MPLS solutions, private Ethernet WANs offer very high performance, with links typically rated at 1 Gbps compared to the 45 Mbps of a traditional T1.

If a WAN combines two or more connection types like if it uses MPLS circuits as well as T3 lines, it can be considered a hybrid WAN. These are useful if the organization wants to provide a cost-effective method to connect their branches together but also have a faster method of transferring important data if needed.

Problems with Wide Area Networks

WAN networks are much more expensive than home or corporate intranets.

WANs that cross international and other territorial boundaries fall under different legal jurisdictions. Disputes can arise between governments over ownership rights and network usage restrictions.

Global WANs require the use of undersea network cables to communicate across continents. Undersea cables are subject to sabotage and also unintentional breaks from ships and weather conditions. Compared to underground landlines, undersea cables tend to take much longer and cost much more to repair.

Storage Area Network

A storage area network (SAN) is a dedicated high-speed network or sub network that interconnects and presents shared pools of storage devices to multiple servers.

A SAN moves storage resources off the common user network and reorganizes them into an independent, high-performance network. This enables each server to access shared storage as if it were a drive directly attached to the server. When a host wants to access a storage device on the SAN, it sends out a block-based access request for the storage device.

A storage area network is typically assembled using three principle components: cabling, host bus adapters (HBAs), and switches attached to storage arrays and servers. Each switch and storage system on the SAN must be interconnected, and the physical interconnections must support bandwidth levels that can adequately handle peak data activities. IT administrators manage storage area networks centrally.

Storage arrays were initially all hard disk drive systems, but are increasingly populated with flash solid-state drives (SSDs).

Uses of Storage Area Networks

Fibre Channel (FC) SANs have the reputation of being expensive, complex and difficult to manage. Ethernet-based iSCSI has reduced these challenges by encapsulating SCSI commands into IP packets that don't require an FC connection.

The emergence of iSCSI means that instead of learning, building and managing two networks -- an Ethernet local area network (LAN) for user communication and an FC SAN for storage -- an organization can use its existing knowledge and infrastructure for both LANs and SANs. This is an especially useful approach in small and midsize businesses that may not have the funds or expertise to support a Fibre Channel SAN.

Organizations use SANs for distributed applications that need fast local network performance. SANs improve the availability of applications through multiple data paths. They can also improve application performance because they enable IT administrators to offload storage functions and segregate networks.

Additionally, SANs help increase the effectiveness and use of storage because they enable administrators to consolidate resources and deliver tiered storage. SANs also improve data protection and security. Finally, SANs can span multiple sites, which helps companies with their business continuity strategies.

Understanding SAN Switches

SAN switches connect servers and pools of shared storage devices. A SAN switch's only job is to move storage traffic. SAN switches are often Fibre Channel switches that are compatible with the FC protocol on which many SANs are based. The switch checks the data packet and identifies its origin and destination. Then, the switch directs the packet to the right storage system. FC switches are meant to be used with high-performance networks.

SAN switches can also be Ethernet based. Such switches should only handle traffic on an IP SAN to keep performance predictable. Ethernet switches deliver traffic to an IP address; they view iSCSI storage targets as IP addresses.

Organizations can combine many switches to build large SAN fabrics that connect many servers and storage ports.

Virtual SAN

A virtual storage area network (VSAN) is a software-defined storage offering that is implemented on top of a hypervisor, such as VMware ESXi or Microsoft Hyper-V. Virtual SANs yield a number of benefits, such as ease of management and scalability.

For the most part, VSANs are hardware-agnostic. As long as the hypervisor recognizes and supports the storage hardware, the VSAN can use it, although each vendor has its own requirements.

Unified SAN

Unified SAN is based on the concept of unified storage, which exposes file storage and block storage through a single storage device, usually a modified network-attached storage appliance (NAS appliance).

A unified SAN takes this concept a step further by exposing not only dedicated logical unit numbers (LUNs) -- like any other SAN -- but file system-based, NAS-like storage.

Converged SAN

Storage area networks are normally kept separate from Ethernet networks. A converged SAN uses a common network infrastructure for network and SAN traffic to eliminate redundant infrastructure and to reduce cost and complexity.

SANs often make use of Fibre Channel, whereas data networks are usually based on Ethernet. Converged SANs adopt Fibre Channel over Ethernet (FCoE), which encapsulates FC payloads into Ethernet frames. Converged SANs are almost always based on 10 Gigabit Ethernet, and multiple network ports are sometimes bonded together to increase throughput.

SAN Pros and Cons

The main benefit of using a SAN is that raw storage is treated as a pool of resources that IT can centrally manage and allocate on an as-needed basis. SANs are also highly scalable because capacity can be added as required.

The main disadvantages of SANs are cost and complexity. SAN hardware tends to be expensive, and building and managing a SAN requires a specialized skill set.

SAN vs. NAS

The terms SAN and NAS are sometimes confused with one another because the acronyms are similar. NAS consists of a storage appliance that is plugged directly into a network switch. Although there are exceptions, NAS appliances are often used as file servers whereas SANs are used for structured data stored in databases.

NAS vs. SAN Storage

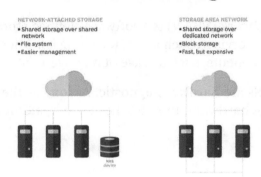

A SAN is far more complex and costly than NAS. A SAN consists of dedicated cabling -- usually Fibre Channel, but Ethernet can be used in iSCSI or FCoE SANs -- dedicated switches and storage hardware. SANs are highly scalable and enable storage to be exposed as LUNs.

In contrast, NAS storage usually exposes storage as a file system, although some NAS appliances support block storage.

Major Vendors and Products

There has been much consolidation in the SAN vendor market, and it is now dominated by some of the largest IT companies.

In September 2016, Dell completed a $60-billion-plus acquisition of EMC in what was the largest IT acquisition ever. EMC was the storage array market leader, and Dell EMC now generates the most revenue and has the broadest storage systems portfolio. Dell EMC storage now includes VMAX, Unity and XtremIO SAN arrays from the old EMC and Compellent from Dell.

Dell's server rival, Hewlett Packard Enterprise (HPE), has also filled out its SAN product portfolio with acquisitions. HPE acquired Nimble Storage in 2017 for $1.2 billion. That followed HPE's $2.35 billion purchase of 3PAR in 2010. The 3PAR and Nimble product lines are now HPE's major SAN array platforms.

NetApp is the largest storage-only vendor remaining following Dell's merger with EMC. NetApp began as Network Appliance in 1992, and it was among the early NAS vendors.

It added block storage capabilities to its FAS (Fabric-Attached Storage) platform in 2002, and FAS arrays are now available with FC, iSCSI or NAS connectivity, or any combination of the three.

IBM and Hitachi Vantara -- previously Hitachi Data Systems -- are the other major SAN array vendors. IBM and Hitachi focus mainly on large enterprises and mainframe-attached storage, although they have broadened their portfolio with flash arrays for open systems. Hitachi Vantara positions its storage arrays to focus on internet of things (IoT) data.

Switching and HBA vendors have also consolidated. Broadcom completed its $5.9 billion acquisition of FC switch vendor Brocade in November 2017. Brocade's major FC rival is Cisco, which is also the leader in Ethernet networking.

The Brocade deal came two years after Broadcom -- then known as Avago -- acquired HBA vendor Emulex Corp. for $606 million in 2015. Cavium acquired Emulex's major HBA rival QLogic for $1 billion in 2016, and it runs QLogic as a wholly owned subsidiary.

System Area Network

A system area network (SAN) is a high-performance, connection-oriented network that can link a cluster of computers. A SAN delivers high bandwidth (1 Gbps or greater) with low latency. A SAN is typically switched by hubs that support eight or more nodes. The cable lengths between nodes on a SAN range from a few meters to a few kilometers.

Unlike existing network technologies such as Ethernet and ATM, a SAN offers a reliable transport service; that is, a SAN guarantees to deliver uncorrupted data in the same order in which it was sent. Connection endpoints in a SAN are not required to use the TCP/IP protocol stack to transfer data unless traffic must be routed between subnets. SAN-local communication can use a native SAN transport, bypassing the TCP/IP protocol stack.

A SAN network interface controller (NIC), a transport driver for the SAN NIC, or a combination of both exposes a private transport interface. However, because most networking applications are written to use TCP/IP through Windows Sockets, they cannot use a SAN directly. The Windows Sockets Direct components shown in the following figure let these applications benefit from using a SAN transparently without requiring modification. Windows Sockets Direct is part of:

- Microsoft Windows 2000 Datacenter Server

- Microsoft Windows 2000 Advanced Server SP2

- Microsoft Windows 2000 Server Appliance Kit SP2

- Microsoft Windows Server 2003

The following figure shows the architecture required to support a SAN. The shaded areas represent components that a SAN NIC vendor supplies to enable using a SAN.

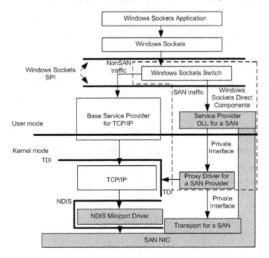

The following is a description of the components shown in this figure.

1. Windows Sockets Application

Application that interfaces with Windows Sockets for network services.

2. Windows Sockets

The Windows Sockets interface (Ws2_32.dll).

3. Windows Sockets SPI

The Windows Sockets service provider interface (SPI).

4. Windows Sockets Switch

The Windows Sockets switches between use of the standard TCP/IP service provider and particular SAN service providers.

5. TCP/IP service Provider

A user-mode DLL and associated kernel-mode proxy driver that comprise the standard base Windows Sockets service provider for TCP/IP. The proxy driver exposes a TDI interface.

6. TCP/IP

The standard TCP/IP protocol driver.

7. San Service Provider

The user-mode DLL portion of the SAN service provider.

Proxy driver for a SAN service provider

The kernel-mode proxy driver of the SAN service provider.

8. NDIS miniport driver

The NDIS miniport driver that supports communication to the SAN NIC using the standard TCP/IP protocol driver.

9. SAN transport

A reliable transport service, which can be fully implemented in the NIC, fully implemented in software, or implemented in a combination of both hardware and software.

10. SAN NIC

The physical SAN network interface controller (NIC).

Passive Optical Local Area Network

A Passive Optical Network (PON) is a point-to-multipoint network using optical splitters and loose tube single mode fiber for outdoor network deployments.

Passive optical network technology has been around for a long time. Outside plant carrier networks (fiber-to-the-home, or FTTH) providers have been using passive optical network technology for over a decade.

PONs work well because their providers have lots of experience with passive optical networks; they know how much bandwidth a customer (one home, or one dwelling unit) typically consumes, so they can set up their split ratios very efficiently. There is a demonstrated blueprint for where to locate splitters, and what ratios are needed. This has been developed through trial and error over time.

The Basics of Passive Optical LANs

A traditional LAN manages signal distribution with numerous routers and switch aggregators. Passive optical LANs use passive optical splitters, just like PONs, but are adapted to indoor network architectures. As an alternative to traditional LAN, passive optical LAN is also a point-to-multipoint network that sends its signals on a strand of single mode fiber. POLAN (or POL) utilizes the optical splitters to divide the high bandwidth signal for multiple users, and makes use of wavelength division multiplexing (WDM) technology to allow for bi-directional upstream and down-stream communication. A passive optical LAN consists of an optical line terminal (OLT) in the main equipment room and optical network terminals (ONTs) located near end-users.

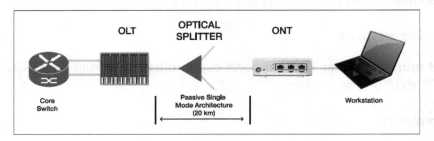

Because of this setup, passive optical LAN can decrease the amount of cable and equipment required to deploy a network. Compared to traditional copper cabling systems and active optical systems, passive optical LAN streamlines the amount of cabling required within a network. Also, because the splitters are passive (requiring no power and emitting no heat), the power and cooling requirements for traditional intermediate distribution frames (IDFs) or telecommunications rooms (TRs) is drastically reduced or eliminated.

Passive Optical LAN Offers Many Benefits

The waters are a bit uncharted when it comes to passive optical LAN, however – especially compared to outdoor PON. As of right now, there are no established POLAN standards; each vendor works from its own platform (ONTs from one vendor are not compatible with the OLTs of another, for example). Also, there is a much shorter history for POLAN deployments; split ratios are generally not as well understood (how much bandwidth does your engineering department really need?). In the past, passive optical LAN deployments were also completed without following a structured approach, so they often lacked interconnection points for future moves, adds and changes (MACs) and repairs.

As a result, the deployment blueprint for POLAN is not as obvious; however, POLAN still offers significant advantages in the right applications. Some of the more favorable fits for POLAN are:

- Hotels
- Campus buildings

- Dormitories
- Hospitals

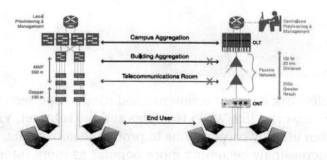

These applications are a good fit because they are environments in which there exists:

- A proliferation of networks requiring convergence.
- A limited amount of space to dedicate to cabling (eliminating some IDFs/TRs that might, for example, provide a hotel with space for another guestroom).
- A potential need for discrete, secure networks.
- A need for easier network support through centralized management.

Enterprise Private Network

An enterprise private network is a computer network that helps enterprise companies with a number of disparate offices connects those offices to each in a secure way over a network. An enterprise private network is mainly set up to share computer resources.

In the U.S., private networks were started in the early 1970s by AT&T. The networks were mainly operated over telecommunications networks. During 1990s as Internet technology evolved, a new type of network called virtual private networks originated. This type of network was built over public infrastructure, and the data was encrypted to protect it from eavesdroppers.

Nowadays, networks built by companies are still called enterprise private networks when privacy is maintained through security procedures and tunneling protocols like Layer 2 Tunneling Protocol.

Some of the advantages of an enterprise private network are:

- The messages are secure because they are encrypted.
- They are cost effective and scalable.

- They help to centralize IT resources.

They enable business continuity.

Virtual Private Network

A Virtual Private Network is a connection method used to add security and privacy to private and public networks, like Wi-Fi Hotspots and the Internet. Virtual Private Networks are most often used by corporations to protect sensitive data. However, using a personal VPN is increasingly becoming more popular as more interactions that were previously face-to-face transition to the Internet. Privacy is increased with a Virtual Private Network because the user's initial IP address is replaced with one from the Virtual Private Network provider. Subscribers can obtain an IP address from any gateway city the VPN service provides. For instance, you may live in San Francisco, but with a Virtual Private Network, you can appear to live in Amsterdam, New York, or any number of gateway cities.

Uses of VPN

- Hide your IP address:

  Connecting to a Virtual Private Network often conceals your real IP address.

- Change your IP address:

  Using a VPN will almost certainly result in getting a different IP address.

- Encrypt data transfers:

  A Virtual Private Network will protect the data you transfer over public Wi-Fi.

- Mask your location:

  With a Virtual Private Network, users can choose the country of origin for their Internet connection.

- Access blocked websites:

  Get around website blocked by governments with a VPN.

Virtual Private Network Security

Security is the main reason why corporations have used VPNs for years. There are increasingly simple methods to intercept data traveling to a network. Wi-Fi spoofing and Firesheep are two easy ways to hack information. A useful analogy is that a firewall protects your data while on the computer and a VPN protects your data on the web. VPNs use advanced encryption protocols and secure tunneling techniques to encapsulate all online data transfers. Most savvy computer users wouldn't dream of connecting to the Internet without a firewall and up-to-date antivirus. Evolving security threats and ever increasing reliance on the Internet make a Virtual Private Network an essential part of well-rounded security. Integrity checks ensure that no data is lost and that the connection has not been hijacked. Since all traffic is protected, VPNs are preferred over proxies.

Setting Up a VPN

Setting up a Virtual Private Network is a straightforward process. It's often as simple as entering a username and sever address. The dominant smartphones can configure Virtual Private Networks using PPTP and L2TP/IPsec protocols. All major operating systems can configure PPTP VPN connections. OpenVPN and L2TP/IPsec protocols require a small open source application (OpenVPN) and certificate download respectively.

Virtual Private Network Protocols

The number of protocols and available security features continue to grow with time. The most common protocols are:

- PPTP - PPTP has been around since the days of Windows 95. The main selling point of PPTP is that it can be simply setup on every major OS. In short, PPTP tunnels a point-to-point connection over the GRE protocol. Unfortunately, the security of the PPTP protocol has been called into question in recent years. It is still strong, but not the most secure.

- L2TP/IPsec - L2TP over IPsec is more secure than PPTP and offers more features. L2TP/IPsec is a way of implementing two protocols together in order to gain the best features of each. For example, the L2TP protocol is used to create a tunnel and IPsec provides a secure channel. These measures make for an impressively secure package.

- Open VPN - OpenVPN is an SSL-based Virtual Private Network that continues to gain popularity. The software used is open source and freely available. SSL is a mature encryption protocol, and OpenVPN can run on a single UDP or TCP port, making it extremely flexible.

References

- Computer-networking, computer-fundamentals: tutorialspoint.com, Retrieved 25 June 2018

- Connecting-personal-level, personal-area: urgentcomm.com, Retrieved 31 March 2018

- Metropolitan-area-network-man: freewimaxinfo.com, Retrieved 11 April 2018

- Wide-area-network-816383: lifewire.com, Retrieved 21 May 2018

- Storage-area-network-SAN: searchstorage.techtarget.com, Retrieved 25 June 2018

- Comparing-passive-optical-networks-and-passive-optical-lans, digital-building: belden.com, Retrieved 09 July 2018

- Enterprise-private-network-26044: techopedia.com, Retrieved 17 July 2018

## 3

Network Infrastructure

Network infrastructure comprises of the essential elements of network nodes such as network interfaces, repeaters and hubs, switches, bridges, modems, routers, etc. Apart from this, it comprises of network links and network structure elements. This chapter closely examines the vital aspects of network infrastructure and includes topics such as firewalls, servers, gateways, proxies, among many others.

A network infrastructure is an interconnected group of computer systems linked by the various parts of a telecommunications architecture. Specifically, this infrastructure refers to the organization of its various parts and their configuration — from individual networked computers to routers, cables, wireless access points, switches, backbones, network protocols, and network access methodologies. Infrastructures can be either open or closed, such as the open architecture of the Internet or the closed architecture of a private intranet. They can operate over wired or wireless network connections, or a combination of both.

The simplest form of network infrastructure typically consists of one or more computers, a network or Internet connection, and a hub to both link the computers to the network connection and tie the various systems to each other. The hub merely links the computers, but does not limit data flow to or from any one system. To control or limit access between systems and regulate information flow, a switch replaces the hub to create network protocols that define how the systems communicate with each other. To allow the network created by these systems to communicate to others, via the network connection, requires a router, which bridges the networks and basically provides a common language for data exchange, according to the rules of each network.

When multiple computers in a single household share the same Internet connection, it is considered a basic form of network infrastructure, whether or not the computers also share information with each other. The Internet itself is a more advanced network infrastructure, in which individual systems access a global network that houses information on various systems, and allows access using web standards and protocols, most commonly framed as web addresses, also known as URLs.

Office intranets are similar to the global Internet, but operate on a closed network infrastructure accessible only by those within it. This generally consists of a central data store — one or more computers known as servers — as well as ethernet cabling, wireless access points, routers, switches, and the individual computers with access to the central data store. The individual computers connect to the network via either cabling or wireless access. The routers and switches then determine what level of access they are allowed to have, and act as traffic directors to point them to the central data store on the servers. As the individual computers send or receive data, the routers ensure it reaches the appropriate place.

Network security is often a primary concern when building a network infrastructure. Most architectures use routers with built-in firewalls, as well as software that allows finely tuned user-access control, data packet monitoring, and strictly defined protocols. Security can also be controlled by adjusting network-sharing properties on individual systems, which limits the folders and files that can be seen by other users on the network.

Network Infrastructure Vulnerabilities

Network infrastructure vulnerabilities are the foundation for all technical security issues in your information systems. These lower-level vulnerabilities affect everything running on your network. That's why you need to test for them and eliminate them whenever possible.

Your focus for ethical hacking tests on your network infrastructure should be to find weaknesses that others can see in your network so you can quantify your network's level of exposure.

Many issues are related to the security of your network infrastructure. Some issues are more technical and require you to use various tools to assess them properly. You can assess others with a good pair of eyes and some logical thinking. Some issues are easy to see from outside the network, and others are easier to detect from inside your network.

When you assess your company's network infrastructure security, you need to look at such areas as:

- Where devices such as a firewall or IPS are placed on the network and how they are configured.

- What hackers see when they perform port scans, and how they can exploit vulnerabilities in your network hosts.

- Network design, such as Internet connections, remote access capabilities, layered defenses, and placement of hosts on the network.

- Interaction of installed security devices such as firewalls, IDSs, and antivirus, and so on.

- What protocols are in use.

- Commonly attacked ports that are unprotected.

- Network host configuration.

- Network monitoring and maintenance.

If a hacker exploits a vulnerability in one of the items above or anywhere in your network's security, bad things can happen:

- A hacker can use a DoS attack, which can take down your Internet connection — or even your entire network.

- A malicious employee using a network analyzer can steal confidential information in e-mails and files being transferred on the network.

- A hacker can set up backdoors into your network.

- A hacker can attack specific hosts by exploiting local vulnerabilities across the network.

Before moving forward with assessing your network infrastructure security, remember to do the following:

- Test your systems from the outside in, the inside out, and the inside in (that is, between internal network segments and DMZs).

- Obtain permission from partner networks that are connected to your network to check for vulnerabilities on their ends that can affect your network's security, such as open ports and lack of a firewall or a misconfigured router.

Choosing Tools

Your tests require the right tools — you need scanners and analyzers, as well as vulnerability assessment tools. Great commercial, shareware, and freeware tools are available.

Just keep in mind that you need more than one tool, and that no tool does everything you need.

If you're looking for easy-to-use security tools with all-in-one packaging, you get what you pay for — most of the time — especially for the Windows platform. Tons of security professionals swear by many free security tools, especially those that run on Linux and other UNIX-based operating systems. Many of these tools offer a lot of value — if you have the time, patience, and willingness to learn their ins and outs.

Scanners and Analyzers

These scanners provide practically all the port-scanning and network-testing tools you'll need:

- Sam Spade for Windows for network queries from DNS lookups to traceroutes.

- SuperScan for ping sweeps and port scanning.

- Essential NetTools for a wide variety of network scanning functionality.

- NetScan Tools Pro for dozens of network security assessment functions, including ping sweeps, port scanning, and SMTP relay testing.

- Getif for SNMP enumeration.

- Nmap or NMapWin which is a happy-clicky-GUI front end to Nmap for host-port probing and operating-system fingerprinting.

- Netcat for security checks such as port scanning and firewall testing.

- LanHound for network analysis.

- WildPackets EtherPeek for network analysis.

Vulnerability Assessment

These vulnerability assessment tools allow you to test your network hosts for various known vulnerabilities as well as potential configuration issues that could lead to security exploits:

- GFI LANguard Network Security Scanner for port scanning and other vulnerability testing.

- Sunbelt Network Security Inspector for vulnerability testing.

- Nessus as a free all-in-one tool for tests like ping sweeps, port scanning, and vulnerability testing.

- Qualys QualysGuard as a great all-in-one tool for in-depth vulnerability testing.

Routers

A router is hardware device designed to receive, analyze and move incoming packets to another network. It may also be used to convert the packets to another network interface, drop them, and perform other actions relating to a network.

Working of Routers

In technical terms, a router is a Layer 3 network gateway device, meaning that it connects two or more networks and that the router operates at the network layer of the OSI model.

Routers contain a processor (CPU), several kinds of digital memory, and input-output

(I/O) interfaces. They function as special-purpose computers, one that does not require a keyboard or display.

The router's memory stores an embedded operating system (O/S). Compared to general-purpose OS products like Microsoft Windows or Apple Mac OS, router operating systems limit what kind of applications can be run on them and also need much smaller amounts of storage space. Examples of popular router operating systems include Cisco Internetwork Operating System (IOS) and DD-WRT. These operating systems are manufactured into a binary firmware image and are commonly called router firmware.

By maintaining configuration information in a part of memory called the routing table, routers also can filter both incoming or outgoing traffic based on the addresses of senders and receivers.

Routers for Business Networks and the Internet

Before home networking became popular, routers could be found only the closets of businesses and schools. Each cost thousands of dollars and require special technical training to set up and manage.

The largest and most powerful network routers from the Internet backbone. These routers must manage many terabits of data flowing through and between Internet Service Provider (ISP) networks.

Home Broadband Routers

Routers became mainstream consumer devices when households began to accumulate multiple computers and wanted to share the home Internet connection.

Home networks use Internet Protocol (IP) routers to connect computers to each other and to the Internet. Early generations of home routers supported wired networking with Ethernet cables while newer wireless routers supported Wi-Fi together with Ethernet. The term broadband router applies to any home wired or wireless router being used for sharing a broadband Internet connection.

Home routers often cost USD $100 or less. They are manufactured to be much more affordable than business routers in part because they offer fewer features. Still, home routers provide many essential home networking functions:

- Sharing of home Internet connections for dozens of devices.
- Basic home network firewall and other security support.
- Ability to change router configuration settings from a Web browsers.

Other Types of Routers and Routing Devices

A class of portable Wi-Fi routers called travel routers are marketed to people and families who want to use the functions of a personal router at other locations besides home.

Routing devices called mobile hotspots that share a mobile (cellular) Internet connection with Wi-Fi clients are also available. Many mobile hotspot devices only work with certain brands of cell service.

Choosing a Router

There are many different types of routers available. From least expensive to top rated, below are some of the routers available.

1. 802.11ac Routers

- Linksys EA6500: This is Linksys first smart Wi-Fi router and gives users total mobile control of the wireless network in their home.

- Netgear AC1750 (R6300): A solid choice for big homes with a lot of wireless devices.

2. 802.11n Routers

- Netgear N300 WNR2000: This is a quality router and the limited lifetime warranty means if you run into any issues while using it, you can contact Netgear to help fix the problem.

- TP-LINK TL-WR841N: TP-LINK routers are some of the most sought after ones on the market. The TL-WR841N features external antennas that make a stronger connection.

3. 802.11g Routers

- Netgear WGR614: The WGR614 is a first-rate router with a wide signal range (ideal for homes with brick walls or similar obstructions). And, a three-year warranty is included.

- Linksys WRT54G Wireless-G: This Linksys router doesn't take any time to install and its strong signal range means you won't have to worry about slow-loading pages.

Functions of a Router (Identify and Describe)

1. Restrict broadcasts to the LAN.
2. Act as the default gateway.

3. Perform Protocol Translation (Wired Ethernet to Wireless/Wi-Fi, or Ethernet to CATV).

4. Move (route) data between networks.

5. Learn and advertise loop free paths.

6. Calculate 'best paths' to reach network destinations.

Restrict Broadcasts to the LAN

Networks (especially Ethernet networks) use broadcast communication at the physical, data link and network layer. Network layer broadcasts are transmissions sent to all hosts using the network layer protocol (usually Internet Protocol [IP] or IPX). Network broadcast communication is used to communicate certain kinds of information that makes the network function (ARP, RARP, DHCP, IPX-SAP broadcasts etc.). Since several devices could attempt to transmit simultaneously and cause collisions, it is preferable to separate large sets of hosts into different broadcast domains using a switch, or router.

As the number of hosts on the network increases, the amount of broadcast traffic increases. If enough broadcast traffic is present on the network, then ordinary communication across the network becomes difficult.

To reduce broadcasts, a network administrator can break up a network with a large number of hosts into two smaller networks. Broadcasts are then restricted to each network, and the router performs as the 'default gateway' to reach the hosts on the other networks.

Act as the Default Gateway

Especially in today's networks, people want to use their computer to connect to the Internet. When your computer wants to talk to a computer on another network, it does so by sending your data to the default gateway. The default gateway is the local router connected to the same network your computer is connected to. The router serving as the default gateway receives your data, looks for the remote address of that far-off computer and makes a routing decision. Based on that routing decision, it forwards your data out a different interface that is closer to that remote computer. There could be several routers between you and the remote computer, so several routers will take part in handing off the packet, much like a fireman's bucket brigade.

Move (route) Data between Networks

Routers have the capability to move data from one network to another. This allows two networks managed by different organizations to exchange data. They create a network between them and exchange data between the routers on that network.

Because a router can accept traffic from any kind of network it is attached to, and forward it to any other network, it can also allow networks that could not normally communicate with each other to exchange data. In technical terms, a token ring network and an ethernet network can communicate over a serial network. Routers make all this possible.

A router can take in an Ethernet frame, strip the ethernet data off, and then drop the IP data into a frame of another type such as SDH/SONET, PDH/T1, ATM, FDDI. In this way a router can also perform 'protocol conversion', provided it has the appropriate hardware and software to support such a function. The whole point, however, is to forward the data from the interface it receives data on, to another interface that retransmits the received data onto another interface serving another network.

Learn and Advertise Loop-Free Paths

Routers can only learn and advertise routes dynamically if they are using a routing protocol such as RIP, OSPF, EIGRP, IS-IS or BGP. Otherwise, a human has to configure the routes by hand, which is called static routing.

Routing moves data on a hop-by-hop basis, what is often called 'hot potato' routing. If a set of routers ends up passing the data around in a circle, without reaching the destination, it's called a 'routing loop'. Packets get handed off around the loop until they die of old age: their 'Time To Live' expires. Time To Live is a counter that is part of the IP datagram header. The Time To Live value is decremented as it passes through each router and eventually it reaches zero and is discarded.

Router Components & Parts

Since routers are just specialized computers, the have the same "parts" as other computers:

- Central Processing Unit (CPU)
- Flash Memory
- Non-Volitile RAM
- RAM
- Network Interfaces
- Console

Central Processing Unit: Runs special software called an "operating system" such as JunOS on Juniper routers, or Cisco IOS (Nexus OS) for Cisco routers. The operating system manages the router's components and provies all the logical networking functions of the router.

Flash Memory is where the operating system is stored, and in this respect, is like the hard disk drive in your computer. If you use a Solid State Disk Drive (SSD), then your computer uses Flash RAM, just like the router does.

Non-Volitile RAM: This is additional memory for storing the backup or startup version of the operating system being used. The router will boot from this memory and load all it's programs from here.

RAM: When the router starts up, the operating system is loaded into RAM. Once the router finishes starting up, it begins to calculate its own routes and, if configured to do so, learns network routes from other routers via RIP (v1 and v2), OSPF, EIGRP, IS-IS or BGP. RAM is also used for caching ARP tables, routing tables, routing metrics and other data that can speed up the process of forwarding of packets.

Network Interfaces: Routers always have lots of network interfaces. The operating system contains 'drivers' that allow the operating system to access the network hardware in the interface modules. Routers will learn which networks are configured on which ports as they start up. After that, they will 'learn' routes from other routers they are connected to, and learn which interface to transmit packets on to reach a remote network destination.

Console: Last, but not least, is the console. In Earlier, managing and configuring a router was performed at the console of individual devices, as was most troubleshooting and diagnostics. Network certification exams will contain a large selection of questions on the configuration and troubleshooting commands you can issue from the console. However, manufacturers are rapidly doing away with a console on each device and building management systems for managing large numbers of network devices from a centralized location.

Hubs

In computer networking, a hub is a small, simple, inexpensive electronic device that joins multiple computers together.

Until the early 2000s, Ethernet hubs were widely used for home networking due to their simplicity and low cost. While broadband routers have replaced them in homes, hubs still serve a useful purpose. Besides Ethernet, a few other types of networks hubs also exist including USB hubs.

Characteristics of Ethernet Hubs

A hub is a rectangular box, often made of plastic, that receives its power from an ordinary wall outlet. A hub joins multiple computers (or other network devices) together to form a single network segment. On this network segment, all computers can communicate directly with each other.

Ethernet hubs vary in the speed (network data rate or bandwidth) they support. Original Ethernet hubs offered only 10 Mbps rated speeds. Newer types of hubs added 100 Mbps support and usually offered both 10 Mbps and 100 Mbps capabilities (so-called dual-speed or 10/100 hubs).

The number of ports an Ethernet hub supports also varies. Four- and five-port Ethernet hubs are most common in home networks, but eight- and 16-port hubs can be found in some home and small office environments. Hubs can be connected to each other to expand the total number of devices a hub network can support.

Older Ethernet hubs were relatively large in size and sometimes noisy as they contained built-in fans for cooling the unit. Modern hub devices are much smaller, designed for mobility, and noiseless.

Passive, Active and Intelligent Hubs

Three basic types of hubs exist:

- passive

- active

- intelligent

Passive hubs do not amplify the electrical signal of incoming packets before broadcasting them out to the network. Active hubs, on the other hand, do perform this amplification, as does a different type of dedicated network device called a repeater. Some people use the terms concentrator when referring to a passive hub and multiport repeater when referring to an active hub.

Intelligent hubs add extra features to an active hub that are of particular importance to businesses. An intelligent hub typically is stackable (built in such a way that multiple units can be placed one on top of the other to conserve space). Intelligent Ethernet hubs also typically include remote management capabilities via SNMP and virtual LAN (VLAN) support.

Working with Ethernet Hubs

To network, a group of computers using an Ethernet hub, first connect an Ethernet cable into the unit, then connect the other end of the cable to each computer's network interface card (NIC). All Ethernet hubs accept the RJ-45 connectors of standard Ethernet cables.

To expand a network to accommodate more devices, Ethernet hubs can also be connected to each other, to switches, or to routers.

When an Ethernet Hub is Needed

Ethernet hubs operate as Layer 1 devices in the OSI model. Although hubs comparable functionality, nearly all mainstream Ethernet network equipment today utilizes network switch technology instead, due to the performance benefits of switches. A hub can be useful for temporarily replacing a broken network switch or when performance is not a critical factor on the network.

Switches

Switches occupy the same place in the network as hubs. Unlike hubs, switches examine each packet and process it accordingly rather than simply repeating the signal to all ports. Switches map the Ethernet addresses of the nodes residing on each network segment and then allow only the necessary traffic to pass through the switch. When a packet is received by the switch, the switch examines the destination and source hardware addresses and compares them to a table of network segments and addresses. If the segments are the same, the packet is dropped or "filtered"; if the segments are different, then the packet is "forwarded" to the proper segment. Additionally, switches prevent bad or misaligned packets from spreading by not forwarding them.

Filtering packets and regenerating forwarded packets enables switching technology to split a network into separate collision domains. The regeneration of packets allows for greater distances and more nodes to be used in the total network design, and dramatically lowers the overall collision rates. In switched networks, each segment is an independent collision domain. This also allows for parallelism, meaning up to one-half of the computers connected to a switch can send data at the same time. In shared networks all nodes reside in a single shared collision domain.

Easy to install, most switches are self-learning. They determine the Ethernet addresses in use on each segment, building a table as packets are passed through the switch. This "plug and play" element makes switches an attractive alternative to hubs.

Switches can connect different network types (such as Ethernet and Fast Ethernet) or networks of the same type. Many switches today offer high-speed links, like Fast Ethernet, which can be used to link the switches together or to give added bandwidth to important servers that get a lot of traffic. A network composed of a number of switches linked together via these fast uplinks is called a "collapsed backbone" network.

Dedicating ports on switches to individual nodes is another way to speed access for critical computers. Servers and power users can take advantage of a full segment for one node, so some networks connect high traffic nodes to a dedicated switch port.

Full duplex is another method to increase bandwidth to dedicated workstations or servers. To use full duplex, both network interface cards used in the server or workstation and the switch must support full duplex operation. Full duplex doubles the potential bandwidth on that link.

Network Congestion

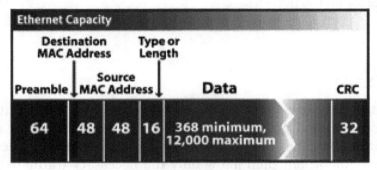

Data Comprises ≈ 70% of the Packet

As more users are added to a shared network or as applications requiring more data are added, performance deteriorates. This is because all users on a shared network are competitors for the Ethernet bus. A moderately loaded 10 Mbps Ethernet network is able to sustain utilization of 35 percent and throughput in the neighborhood of 2.5 Mbps after accounting for packet overhead, inter-packet gaps and collisions. A moderately loaded Fast Ethernet or Gigabit Ethernet shares 25 Mbps or 250 Mbps of real data in the same circumstances. With shared Ethernet and Fast Ethernet, the likelihood of collisions increases as more nodes and/or more traffic is added to the shared collision domain.

Ethernet itself is a shared media, so there are rules for sending packets to avoid conflicts and protect data integrity. Nodes on an Ethernet network send packets when they determine the network is not in use. It is possible that two nodes at different locations could try to send data at the same time. When both PCs are transferring a packet to the network at the same time, a collision will result. Both packets are retransmitted, adding to the traffic problem. Minimizing collisions is a crucial element in the design and operation of networks. Increased collisions are often the result of too many users or too much traffic on the network, which results in a great deal of contention for network bandwidth. This can slow the performance of the network from the user's point of view. Segmenting, where a network is divided into different pieces joined together logically with switches or routers, reduces congestion in an overcrowded network by eliminating the shared collision domain.

Collision rates measure the percentage of packets that are collisions. Some collisions are inevitable, with less than 10 percent common in well-running networks.

The Factors Affecting Network Efficiency
• Amount of traffic
• Number of nodes
• Size of packets
• Network diameter

Measuring Network Efficiency
• Average to peak load deviation
• Collision Rate
• Utilization Rate

Utilization rate is another widely accessible statistic about the health of a network. This statistic is available in Novell's console monitor and WindowsNT performance monitor as well as any optional LAN analysis software. Utilization in an average network above 35 percent indicates potential problems. This 35 percent utilization is near optimum, but some networks experience higher or lower utilization optimums due to factors such as packet size and peak load deviation.

A switch is said to work at "wire speed" if it has enough processing power to handle full Ethernet speed at minimum packet sizes. Most switches on the market are well ahead of network traffic capabilities supporting the full "wire speed" of Ethernet, 14,480 pps (packets per second), and Fast Ethernet, 148,800 pps.

General Benefits of Network Switching

Switches replace hubs in networking designs, and they are more expensive. So why is the desktop switching market doubling ever year with huge numbers sold? The price of switches is declining precipitously, while hubs are a mature technology with small price declines. This means that there is far less difference between switch costs and hub costs than there used to be, and the gap is narrowing.

Since switches are self-learning, they are as easy to install as a hub. Just plug them in and go. And they operate on the same hardware layer as a hub, so there are no protocol issues.

There are two reasons for switches being included in network designs. First, a switch breaks one network into many small networks so the distance and repeater limitations are restarted. Second, this same segmentation isolates traffic and reduces collisions relieving network congestion. It is very easy to identify the need for distance and repeater extension, and to understand this benefit of network switching. But the second benefit, relieving network congestion, is hard to identify and harder to understand the degree by which switches will help performance. Since all switches add small latency delays to packet processing, deploying switches unnecessarily can actually slow down network performance.

Network Switching

The benefits of switching vary from network to network. Adding a switch for the first time has different implications than increasing the number of switched ports already installed. Understanding traffic patterns is very important to network switching – the goal being to eliminate (or filter) as much traffic as possible. A switch installed in a location where it forwards almost all the traffic it receives will help much less than one that filters most of the traffic.

Networks that are not congested can actually be negatively impacted by adding switches. Packet processing delays, switch buffer limitations, and the retransmissions that can result sometimes slows performance compared with the hub-based alternative. If your network is not congested, don't replace hubs with switches. How can you tell if performance problems are the result of network congestion? Measure utilization factors and collision rates.

Good Candidates for Performance Boosts from Switching

- Utilization more than 35%
- Collision rates more than 10%

Utilization load is the amount of total traffic as a percent of the theoretical maximum for the network type, 10 Mbps in Ethernet, 100 Mbps in Fast Ethernet. The collision rate is the number of packets with collisions as a percentage of total packages.

Network response times (the user-visible part of network performance) suffers as the load on the network increases, and under heavy loads small increases in user traffic often results in significant decreases in performance. This is similar to automobile freeway dynamics, in that increasing loads results in increasing throughput up to a point, then further increases in demand results in rapid deterioration of true throughput. In Ethernet, collisions increase as the network is loaded, and this causes retransmissions and increases in load which cause even more collisions. The resulting network overload slows traffic considerably.

Using network utilities found on most server operating systems network managers can determine utilization and collision rates. Both peak and average statistics should be considered.

Replacing a Central Hub with a Switch

This switching opportunity is typified by a fully shared network, where many users are connected in cascading hub architecture. The two main impacts of switching will be faster network connection to the server(s) and the isolation of non-relevant traffic from each segment. As the network bottleneck is eliminated performance grows until a new system bottleneck is encountered – such as maximum server performance.

Adding Switches to a Backbone Switched Network

Congestion on a switched network can usually be relieved by adding more switched ports, and increasing the speed of these ports. Segments experiencing congestion are identified by their utilization and collision rates, and the solution is either further segmentation or faster connections. Both Fast Ethernet and Ethernet switch ports are added further down the tree structure of the network to increase performance.

Designing for Maximum Benefit

Changes in network design tend to be evolutionary rather than revolutionary-rarely is a network manager able to design a network completely from scratch. Usually, changes are made slowly with an eye toward preserving as much of the usable capital investment as possible while replacing obsolete or outdated technology with new equipment.

Fast Ethernet is very easy to add to most networks. A switch or bridge allows Fast Ethernet to connect to existing Ethernet infrastructures to bring speed to critical links. The faster technology is used to connect switches to each other, and to switched or shared servers to ensure the avoidance of bottlenecks.

Many client/server networks suffer from too many clients trying to access the same server, which creates a bottleneck where the server attaches to the LAN. Fast Ethernet, in combination with switched Ethernet, creates the perfect cost-effective solution for avoiding slow client server networks by allowing the server to be placed on a fast port.

Distributed processing also benefits from Fast Ethernet and switching. Segmentation of the network via switches brings big performance boosts to distributed traffic networks, and the switches are commonly connected via a Fast Ethernet backbone.

Good Candidates for Performance Boosts from Switching

- Important to know network demand per node.
- Try to group users with the nodes they communicate with most often on the same segment.
- Look for departmental traffic patterns.
- Avoid switch bottlenecks with fast uplinks.

- Move users switch between segments in an iterative process until all nodes seeing less than 35% utilization.

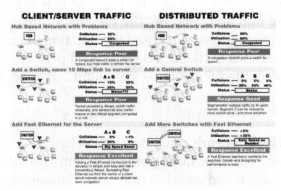

Advanced Switching Technology

Management provides benefits in many networks. Large networks with mission critical applications are managed with many sophisticated tools, using SNMP to monitor the health of devices on the network. Networks using SNMP or RMON (an extension to SNMP that provides much more data while using less network bandwidth to do so) will either manage every device, or just the more critical areas. VLANs are another benefit to management in a switch. A VLAN allows the network to group nodes into logical LANs that behave as one network, regardless of physical connections. The main benefit is managing broadcast and multicast traffic. An unmanaged switch will pass broadcast and multicast packets through to all ports. If the network has logical grouping that are different from physical groupings then a VLAN-based switch may be the best bet for traffic optimization.

Another benefit to management in the switches is Spanning Tree Algorithm. Spanning Tree allows the network manager to design in redundant links, with switches attached in loops. This would defeat the self-learning aspect of switches, since traffic from one node would appear to originate on different ports. Spanning Tree is a protocol that allows the switches to coordinate with each other so that traffic is only carried on one of the redundant links (unless there is a failure, then the backup link is automatically activated). Network managers with switches deployed in critical applications may want to have redundant links. In this case management is necessary. But for the rest of the networks an unmanaged switch would do quite well, and is much less expensive.

Store-and-Forward vs. Cut-Through

LAN switches come in two basic architectures, cut-through and store-and-forward. Cut-through switches only examine the destination address before forwarding it on to its destination segment. A store-and-forward switch, on the other hand, accepts and analyzes the entire packet before forwarding it to its destination. It takes more time to examine the entire packet, but it allows the switch to catch certain packet errors and collisions and keep them from propagating bad packets through the network.

Today, the speed of store-and-forward switches has caught up with cut-through switches to the point where the difference between the two is minimal. Also, there are a large number of hybrid switches available that mix both cut-through and store-and-forward architectures.

Blocking vs Non-Blocking Switches

Take a switch's specifications and add up all the ports at theoretical maximum speed, then you have the theoretical sum total of a switch's throughput. If the switching bus, or switching components cannot handle the theoretical total of all ports the switch is considered a "blocking switch". There is debate whether all switches should be designed non-blocking, but the added costs of doing so are only reasonable on switches designed to work in the largest network backbones. For almost all applications, a blocking switch that has an acceptable and reasonable throughput level will work just fine.

Consider an eight port 10/100 switch. Since each port can theoretically handle 200 Mbps (full duplex) there is a theoretical need for 1600 Mbps, or 1.6 Gbps. But in the real world each port will not exceed 50% utilization, so a 800 Mbps switching bus is adequate. Consideration of total throughput versus total ports demand in the real world loads provides validation that the switch can handle the loads of your network.

Switch Buffer Limitations

As packets are processed in the switch, they are held in buffers. If the destination segment is congested, the switch holds on to the packet as it waits for bandwidth to become available on the crowded segment. Buffers that are full present a problem. So some analysis of the buffer sizes and strategies for handling overflows is of interest for the technically inclined network designer.

In real world networks, crowded segments cause many problems, so their impact on switch consideration is not important for most users, since networks should be designed to eliminate crowded, congested segments. There are two strategies for handling full buffers. One is "backpressure flow control" which sends packets back upstream to the source nodes of packets that find a full buffer. This compares to the strategy of simply dropping the packet, and relying on the integrity features in networks to retransmit automatically. One solution spreads the problem in one segment to other segments, propagating the problem. The other solution causes retransmissions, and that resulting increase in load is not optimal. Neither strategy solves the problem, so switch vendors use large buffers and advise network managers to design switched network topologies to eliminate the source of the problem – congested segments.

Layer 3 Switching

A hybrid device is the latest improvement in internetworking technology. Combining the packet handling of routers and the speed of switching, these multilayer switches operate on both layer 2 and layer 3 of the OSI network model. The performance of this class of switch is aimed at the core of large enterprise networks. Sometimes called routing switches or IP switches, multilayer switches look for common traffic flows, and switch these flows on the hardware layer for speed. For traffic outside the normal flows, the multilayer switch uses routing functions. This keeps the higher overhead routing functions only where it is needed, and strives for the best handling strategy for each network packet.

Many vendors are working on high-end multilayer switches, and the technology is definitely a "work in process". As networking technology evolves, multilayer switches are likely to replace routers in most large networks.

Network Bridges

Like repeaters, bridges are used to connect similar LANs together, for example, Ethernet-to-Ethernet and operate at the bottom two layers of the OSI model, i.e. physical layer and data link layer. As it operates on second layer of the OSI model,' it relays only necessary data to other signals. MAC addresses (physical addresses) are used to determine whether data is necessary or not.

It passes information from one LAN segment to another based on the destination address of the packet. In other words, when a bridge receives data through one of its ports, it checks the data for a MAC address. If this address matches that of the node connected to other port, the bridge sends this data through this port. This action is called forwarding. If the address does not match with any node connected to other port, the bridge discards it. This action is called filtering. Unlike repeaters, bridges have buffers to store and forward packets in the event that the destination link is congested with traffic.

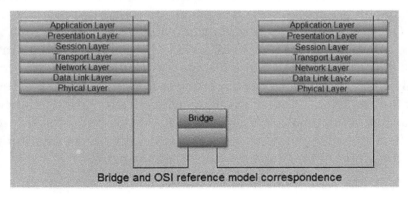

Bridge and OSI reference model correspondence

The main advantage of bridge over repeater is that it has filtering action. If any noise on Ethernet occurs because of collision or disturbance in electrical signal, the bridge will consider it as an incorrectly formed frame and win not forward to the segment connected to other port of the bridge. Note that bridge can relay broadcast packets and packets with unknown destination.

So far, we have seen that at the maximum four repeaters can be used to connect multiple Ethernet segments. However, if a bridge is provided between repeaters, this limit of four is increased. The maximum number of bridges is not specifically limited.

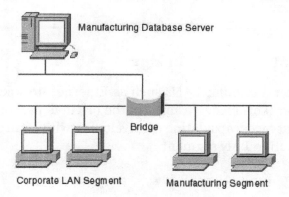

Manufacturing Database Server

Bridge

Corporate LAN Segment   Manufacturing Segment

From architecture point of view bridges are protocol independent devices and are very simple. They do not perform complex processes on the data packets traveling through them such as the evaluation of the network as a whole in order to make end-to-end routing decisions. They simply read the destination address of the incoming data packet and forward it along its way to the next link. Therefore, bridges are Inexpensive and fast. There are bridges called cascading bridges, and are used to support multiple LANs connected by multiple media.

Dissimilar LANs such as Ethernet-to-token ring can also be connected with the help of bridge known as encapsulating bridge. The function of encapsulating bridge is also very simple. It encapsulates the originating LAN data along with control information of the end user LAN. Bridges with routing function between LANs are also available.

Computer 1 wishes to talk to computer 3 on the same network. The packet sent by computer 1 will contain the physical address of computer 3 that will also be received by the bridge device connecting the two LAN segments. The bridge will read the physical address contained in the packet and observe that this address belongs to the computer on the same LAN segment. Hence, bridge will filter this packet and will not allow it to be transmitted on other side of the network. In case computer 1 wishes to talk with computer C on other segment, the bridge will know from its table of addresses that this address belongs to the computer attached to other segment of the network. In this case this will be forwarded to the other segment of the LAN. The bridge learns location of computers attached the network by watching frames. This will be explained liter on in the subsequent discussion. Note that case of broadcast and multicast packets, bridge forwards these packets to all computers attached to the segment on both sides.

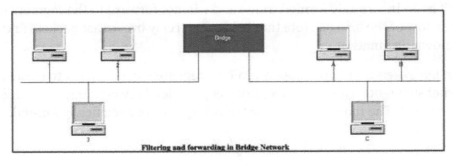

Filtering and forwarding in Bridge Network

Media Access Control (MAC) Bridge

This is used to connect dissimilar LANs such as Ethernet -to-token ring using encapsulation or translation. This bridge translates the original' packet format from the requesting LAN segment by encapsulating or enveloping with control data specific to the protocol of the destination LAN segment.

Address Table

As explained above, each bridge should have an address table that indicates the location of different computers or nodes on the segments of LAN. More specifically, it indicates the connection between nodes and ports. When a bridge is booted first time, this table is found to be blank. Now, this question arises how this table is filled with appropriate addresses of different nodes attached to ports. Most of the bridges are called adaptive or self-leaning bridges because they learn the location of the node and associated port themselves and make a list of nodes attached to each segment.

When a bridge receives a data packet from a computer, it first copies the physical address of that computer contained in the packet into its list. Afterward, bridge determines whether this packet should be forwarded or not. In other words, the bridge learns the location of the computer on the network as soon as the computer on the network sends some packet.

If a computer does not send a packet, the bridge will never be able to determine its position and unnecessarily forward the packet on network. Fortunately, this cannot happen because a computer with network software attached to a network transmits at least one frame when the system first boots. Furthermore, computer communication being bidirectional, there is always an acknowledgement for each received packets.

Bridge Protocols

Bridge protocols include spanning tree, source routing protocol, and source routing transparent.

Spanning Tree Protocol (STP) Bridge

This is also known as adaptive or self-learning bridges and is defined in IEEE 802.1 standards. Ideally, in bridged network, the network tree of the bridge provides only one span (link) for each LAN-to-LAN connection and therefore, no network with bridges can form a loop. Sometimes, looping can occur.

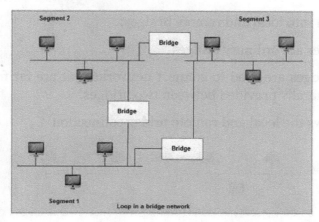

A broadcast data packet sent by the computer attached on segment 1can reach to all computers attached on segment 2 and 3 without a connection between segment 1 and 3. Sometimes, the bridge connection between segment 1and 3 or like is provided to give the network more redundancy. Now, in this case the same broadcast packet sent by the segment 1 will reach to segment 3 by two routes i.e. from segment 1 to 2 to 3 and another by segment 1 to 3. In this manner the computers on segment 3 will receive duplicate packets. In case of large networks some segments may receive many packets and thus cause looping.

A loop, therefore, can cause a broadcast packet or a packet with an unknown destination to circulate through it, thus rendering the network inoperable. This condition is avoided by making some bridges not to forward frames. An algorithm known as distributed spanning tree (DST) accomplishes this task. This algorithm decides which bridge should forward the packets in the network. Under this scheme bridges exchange a control message known as a hello message to select a single transmission route. Remaining bridges maintain a standby position and provide alternate path in case of the same bridge fails in the selected transmission path. Bridge connecting segment 1 and 3 will be active only if the bridge connecting segment 2 and 3 fails otherwise it acts as a standby bridge for network. In other words, bridges that support the spanning tree algorithm have the ability to automatically reconfigure themselves for alternate paths if a network segment fails, thereby improving overall reliability.

IBM Source Routing Protocol (SRP) Bridge

These are programmed with specific routes for each packet based on considerations such as the physical location of the nodes, and the number of bridges involved.

Source Routing Transparent (SRT)

It is defined in theIEEE802.1 standard. It is effectively a combination of STP and SRP. The SRT router can connect LANs by either method, as programmed.

Classification of Bridges

These are classified into local and remote bridges:

- Local bridges are ordinary bridges.

- Remote bridges are used to connect networks that are far from each other. A WAN is generally provided between two bridges.

- Figure shows the local and remote bridge connection.

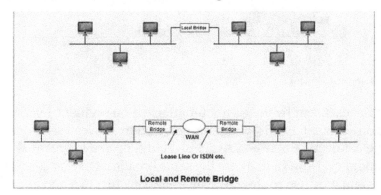

Local and Remote Bridge

Gateways

A gateway is a node (router) in a computer network, a key stopping point for data on its way to or from other networks. Thanks to gateways, we are able to communicate and send data back and forth. The Internet wouldn't be any use to us without gateways (as well as a lot of other hardware and software).

In a workplace, the gateway is the computer that routes traffic from a workstation to the outside network that is serving up the Web pages. For basic Internet connections at home, the gateway is the Internet Service Provider that gives you access to the entire Internet.

A node is simply a physical place where the data stops for either transporting or reading/using. (A computer or modem is a node; a computer cable isn't.) Here are a few node notes:

- On the Internet, the node that's a stopping point can be a gateway or a host node.

- A computer that controls the traffic your Internet Service Provider (ISP) receives is a node.

If you have a wireless network at home that gives your entire family access to the Internet, your gateway is the modem (or modem-router combo) your ISP provides so you can connect to their network. On the other end, the computer that controls all of the data traffic your Internet Service Provider (ISP) takes and sends out is itself a node.

When a computer-server acts as a gateway, it also operates as a firewall and a proxy server. A firewall keeps out unwanted traffic and outsiders off a private network. A proxy server is software that "sits" between programs on your computer that you use (such as a Web browser) and a computer server—the computer that serves your network. The proxy server's task is to make sure the real server can handle your online data requests.

Router as Gateway

A gateway is often associated with a router. A router is hardware—a small piece of computer/network-related equipment that connects you to the Internet. In home networks, the router comes with special software that you install on one computer. You're then able to use the software to set up your home network so everyone allowed on your network can connect to the ISP and the Internet. A router can be connected to two or more networks at a time, but for home networks that's generally not the case.

When you do a Google search or compose an email and hit "Send," your computer sends the data to your router. Your router then, which is hardwired to do its job right, figures out the next destination of the data based on its "comprehension" of the condition of the networks.

Routers can be gateways because a router can control the path through which information is sent in and out. It does so by using built-in headers and forwarding tables to figure out where packets of data need to be sent. Those packets of data carry your emails, transactions, online activity and so on.

A gateway is one of the many ways our data is moved over the Web for us. The gateway gives us entry into different networks so we can send email, look at Web pages, buy things online, and more. You can easily say that gateways deliver the freedom, information and convenience we enjoy online.

Gateways can take several forms and perform a variety of tasks. These include:

- Web application firewall - filters traffic to and from a web server and look at application-layer data.

- API, SOA or XML gateway - manages traffic flowing into and out of a service, micro services-oriented architecture or an XML-based web service.

- IoT gateway - aggregates sensor data, translates between sensor protocols, processes sensor data before sending it onward and more.

- Cloud storage gateway - translates storage requests with various cloud storage service API calls.

- Media gateway - converts data from the format required for one type of network to the format required for another.

- Amazon API Gateway - allows a developer to connect non-AWS applications to AWS back-end resources.

- VoIP trunk gateway - facilitates the use of plain old telephone service (POTS) equipment, such as landline phones and fax machines, with a voice over IP (VoIP) network.

- Email security gateway - prevents the transmission of emails that break company policy or will transfer information with malicious intent.

Proxies

Proxy server is an intermediary server between client and the internet. Proxy servers offers the following basic functionalities:

- Firewall and network data filtering.

- Network connection sharing.

- Data caching.

Proxy servers allow to hide, conceal and make your network id anonymous by hiding your IP address.

Purpose of Proxy Servers

Following are the reasons to use proxy servers:

- Monitoring and Filtering

- Improving performance

- Translation

- Accessing services anonymously

- Security

Monitoring and Filtering

Proxy servers allow us to do several kind of filtering such as:

- Content Filtering
- Filtering encrypted data
- Bypass filters
- Logging and eavesdropping

Improving Performance

It fastens the service by process of retrieving content from the cache which was saved when previous request was made by the client.

Translation

It helps to customize the source site for local users by excluding source content or substituting source content with original local content. In this the traffic from the global users is routed to the source website through Translation proxy.

Accessing services Anonymously

In this the destination server receives the request from the anonym zing proxy server and thus does not receive information about the end user.

Security

Since the proxy server hides the identity of the user hence it protects from spam and the hacker attacks.

Architecture

The proxy server architecture is divided into several modules as shown in the following diagram:

Proxy User Interface

This module controls and manages the user interface and provides an easy to use graphical interface, window and a menu to the end user. This menu offers the following functionalities:

- Start proxy
- Stop proxy
- Exit
- Blocking URL
- Blocking client
- Manage log
- Manage cache
- Modify configuration

Proxy server listener

It is the port where new request from the client browser is listened. This module also performs blocking of clients from the list given by the user.

Connection Manager

It contains the main functionality of the proxy server. It performs the following functions:

- Read request from header of the client.
- Parse the URL and determine whether the URL is blocked or not.
- Generate connection to the web server.
- Read the reply from the web server.
- If no copy of page is found in the cache then download the page from web server else will check its last modified date from the reply header and accordingly will read from the cache or server from the web.
- Then it will also check whether caching is allowed or not and accordingly will cache the page.

Cache Manager

This module is responsible for storing, deleting, clearing and searching of web pages in the cache.

Log Manager

This module is responsible for viewing, clearing and updating the logs.

Configuration

This module helps to create configuration settings, which in turn let other modules to perform desired configurations such as caching.

Servers

A server is a computer designed to process requests and deliver data to another computer over the internet or a local network.

The word "server" is understood by most to mean a web server where webpages can be accessed over the internet through a client like a web browser. However, there are several types of servers, including local ones like file servers that store data within an intranet network.

Although any computer running the necessary software can function as a server, the most typical use of the word references the enormous, high-powered machines that function as the pumps pushing and pulling data from the internet.

Most computer networks support one or more servers that handle specialized tasks. As a rule, the larger the network in terms of clients that connect to it or the amount of data that it moves, the more likely it is that several servers play a role, each dedicated to a specific purpose.

Strictly speaking, the server is the software that handles a specific task. However, the powerful hardware that supports this software is also usually called a server because server software coordinating a network of hundreds or thousands of clients requires hardware much more robust than what you'd buy for ordinary consumer use.

Common Types of Servers

While some dedicated servers focus on one function only, some implementations use one server for multiple purposes.

A large, general-purpose network that supports a medium-sized company likely deploys several types of servers, including:

- Web server: Web servers show pages and run apps through web browsers. The server your browser is connected to right now is a web server that's delivering this page and any images you see on it. The client program, in this case, is most likely a browser like Internet Explorer, Chrome, Firefox, Opera, or Safari. Web servers are used for all sorts of things in addition to delivering simple text and images, such as for uploading and backing up files online through a cloud storage service or online backup service.

- Email server: Email servers facilitate the sending and receiving of email messages. If you have an email client on your computer, the software is connecting to an IMAP or POP email server to download your messages to your computer, and an SMTP server to send messages back through the email server.

- FTP server: FTP servers support the moving of files through File Transfer Protocol tools. FTP servers are accessible remotely via FTP client programs.

- Identity Server: Identity servers support logins and security roles for authorized users.

Hundreds of different types of specialized server types support computer networks. Apart from the common corporate types, home users often interface with online game servers, chat servers, and audio and video streaming servers, among others.

Network Server Types

Many networks on the internet employ a client-server networking model that integrates websites and communication services.

An alternative model, called peer-to-peer networking, allows all the devices on a network to function as either a server or client on an as-needed basis. Peer networks offer a greater degree of privacy because communication between computers is narrowly targeted, but most implementations of peer-to-peer networking aren't robust enough to support large traffic spikes.

Server Clusters

The word cluster is used broadly in computer networking to refer to an implementation of shared computing resources. Typically, a cluster integrates the resources of two or more computing devices that could otherwise function separately for some common purpose (often a workstation or server device).

A web server farm is a collection of networked web servers, each with access to content on the same site. They function as a cluster conceptually. However, purists debate the technical classification of a server farm as a cluster, depending on the details of the hardware and software configuration.

Servers at Home

Because servers are just software, people can run servers at home, accessible only to devices attached to their home network. For example, some network-aware hard drives use the Network Attached Storage server protocol to allow different PCs on the home network to access a shared set of files.

Plex media server software helps users consume digital media on TVs and entertainment devices regardless of whether the media files are on the cloud or a local PC.

More Information on Servers

Since uptime is critically important for most servers, they never shut down but instead run 24/7.

However, servers sometimes go down intentionally for scheduled maintenance, which is why some websites and services notify their users of "scheduled downtime" or "scheduled maintenance." Servers might also go down unintentionally during something like a DDoS attack.

Firewalls

In computing, a firewall is software or firmware that enforces a set of rules about what data packets will be allowed to enter or leave a network. Firewalls are incorporated into a wide variety of networked devices to filter traffic and lower the risk that malicious packets traveling over the public internet can impact the security of a private network. Firewalls may also be purchased as stand-alone software applications.

The term firewall is a metaphor that compares a type of physical barrier that's put in place to limit the damage a fire can cause, with a virtual barrier that's put in place to limit damage from an external or internal cyber attack. When located at the perimeter of a network, firewalls provide low-level network protection, as well as important logging and auditing functions.

While the two main types of firewalls are host-based and network-based, there are many different types that can be found in different places and controlling different activities. A host-based firewall is installed on individual servers and monitors incoming and outgoing signals. A network-based firewall can be built into the cloud's infrastructure, or it can be a virtual firewall service.

Major Types of Firewalls

Traditional Network Firewall

Packet-filtering network firewalls provide essential network protection by helping to prevent unwanted traffic from getting in to the corporate network. They work by applying a set of network firewall security rules to decide whether to allow or deny access to the network. Typical rules include: denying entry to all traffic except for traffic destined for specific ports corresponding to specific application running inside the corporate network; and allowing or denying access to data using specific protocols or from specific IP addresses.

- Protection level: High. The vast majority of network compromises are caused by malicious data gaining access to the corporate network from outside, and a traditional firewall can help prevent this by controlling access to the network. But firewalls are only as effective as the staff that manages them: about 99% of firewall breaches are caused by simple misconfigurations rather than flaws in the firewall itself.

- Strengths and weaknesses: The availability of open source firewall software that runs on standard hardware means that a network firewall solution can be built at very low cost. A traditional network firewall is also only as effective as the rules that it applies, so a firewall configured with ineffective or outdated rules will let in traffic that should be excluded.

- Do you need it? : All corporate networks need some form of firewall to control the data that attempts to flow on to it. An alternative to a traditional firewall is a next-generation firewall (NGFW) that can inspect the contents of packets to give administrators far greater control over the traffic that is allowed to enter and leave the network.

- Vendors: Barracuda, Check Point Software, Cisco, Sophos, Juniper Networks, Palo Alto Networks.

- Open source firewall software: pfSense, Untangle, Smoothwall Express.

Next-generation Firewalls (NGFWs)

Next-generation firewalls serve the same purpose as traditional firewalls – protecting the network from unwanted data traffic – but they work in a different way to achieve this. Specifically, NGFWs offer application awareness with full stack visibility by looking at the contents of each data packet, rather than just its port, source and destination IP address, and protocol. By using an application layer firewall, this enables you to ban the use of specific applications, such as peer-to-peer file sharing applications, or to restrict how applications are used, for example, by allowing Skype to be used for voice over IP calls, but not for file sharing.

- Protection level: Very high, because of the high level of granular control they provide. These capabilities may be required for PCI or HIPAA compliance.

- Strengths and weaknesses: NGFWs provide far more granular control over what data is and is not allowed to access the corporate network, allowing NGFWs to mitigate a wider range of possible threats. But NGFWs are more expensive than traditional firewalls, and because they carry out packet inspection rather than simple packet filtering they have a more limited data through put which can cause network performance issues.

- Do you need it? Leaving cost and performance issues to one side, a NGFW provides better network firewall protection than a traditional firewall. Most NGFWs also provide other optional security features such as an intrusion detection system, malware scanning, and SSL data inspection. These can be valuable to companies that do not already have point solutions providing these features, but they also can cause the data throughput capability of the NGFW to drop significantly when activated.

- Vendors: Barracuda, Check Point Software, Cisco, Sophos, Juniper Networks, Palo Alto Networks

Web Application Firewalls

A web application firewall is usually a proxy server that stands between an application running on a server and the application's users who access the application from outside the corporate network. The proxy server accepts incoming data and then establishes its own connection to the application on behalf of the external user. A key benefit of this setup is that the application is shielded from port scans, attempts to determine the software running on the application server, or other malicious activity directed by end users at the application. The proxy server also analyzes the data to filter malicious requests (such as deliberately malformed requests designed to result in the execution of malicious code), preventing them from ever reaching the web application server.

- Protection level: High, because they provide a buffer between the web application server and unknown and possibly malicious users out on the internet who could otherwise gain access to the web application server directly. This is important because many applications hold confidential data that is valuable to hackers, making web-facing applications a particularly attractive target.

- Strengths and weaknesses: Web application firewalls are simpler and less prone to security vulnerabilities than web application servers themselves, and more easily patched. That means they can make it significantly harder for hackers to reach applications behind the firewall. But not all applications are easily supported by proxy firewalls, and they can reduce the performance of the protected application to end-users.

- Do you need it? Web applications are designed to be accessed from the Internet, so they are likely to receive a large quantity of connections originating from it. For that reason, many organizations take the view that while their networks are best protected by a conventional packet filtering firewall or a next-generation firewall, it makes more sense to send web application traffic to the application through a dedicated application firewall.

- Vendors: F5 Networks, Fortinet, Barracuda, Citrix, Imperva.

Database Firewalls

As the name suggests, database firewalls are a subset of web application firewalls designed to protect databases. They are usually installed directly in front of the database server they protect (or near the network gateway when they are designed to protect more than one database running on more than one server). They are designed to detect and prevent specific database attacks, such as cross-site scripting, that can lead to attackers accessing confidential information stored on the databases.

- Protection level: High. Corporate data tends to be extremely valuable, and the loss of confidential information is usually expensive and costly in terms of lost reputation and bad publicity. For that reason, it is necessary to take all reasonable steps to protect databases and the data they contain. A database firewall adds significantly to the security of this stored data.

- Do you need it? If you maintain databases containing valuable or confidential information, then the use of a database firewall is highly advisable. In 2016, over 4 billion records were stolen from databases, according to Risk Based Security, four times as many as in 2013. As hackers appear to be successfully targeting databases, that means protecting records is becoming more important than ever.

- Strengths and weaknesses: Database firewalls can be an effective security measure, and they can also be used to monitor and audit database accesses, and to produce compliance reports for regulatory purposes. However, they are only effective if they are correctly configured and updated, and offer little protection against zero-day exploits.

- Vendors: Oracle, Imperva, Fortinet.

Unified Threat Management (UTM) Appliances

Unified threat management (UTM) appliances provide a nearly complete security solution for small- and medium-sized business in the form of a single box that plugs in to the network. Typical UTM features include a traditional firewall, an intrusion detection system , internet gateway security (which includes scanning incoming traffic such as emails for viruses and other malware or malicious attachments, and web address blacklisting to prevent employees from visiting known malicious sites such as phishing sites), and they sometimes contain web application firewall and next-generation firewall (NGFW) features as well.

- Protection level: Medium. Most UTMs do a good job securing a network, but best-of-breed solutions for each security function are likely to offer better protection.

- Do you need it? UTMs are ideal for smaller organizations that do not have dedicated security staff and lack the skills needed to configure point solutions.

- Strengths and weaknesses: The key attraction of UTMs is simplicity: a single purchase covers every security need, and all the security features can be controlled and configured from a single management console. Some UTMs offer a base level of security in the initial purchase price, and extra security services (such as IPS) can be enabled for an additional license fee. Although the key drawback is that UTMs may not provide the same level of protection as a combination of more complex products, this may be academic because often the choice is between having a UTM and having no security solution at all.

- Vendors: Leading UTM vendors include Fortinet, SonicWALL, Juniper Networks, Check Point Software, WatchGuard and Sophos.

Cloud-based Firewalls

A cloud-based firewall is an alternative to a firewall running in the corporate data center, but its purpose is exactly the same: to protect a network, application, database, or other IT resources.

- Protection level: High. A cloud firewall provided as a service is configured and maintained by security professionals who specialize in firewall management, so it is capable of offering very good levels of protection for the assets it is protecting. It is also likely to be highly available with little or no scheduled or unscheduled downtime. They are usually implemented by configuring corporate routers to divert traffic to the cloud-based firewall, while mobile users either connect to it via a VPN or by using it as a proxy.

- Do you need it? Cloud-based firewalls are particularly attractive to large organizations, which lack sufficient security personnel, as well as companies with multiple sites or branch offices that need protecting. The market for cloud-based firewalls is growing strongly and is expected to reach $2.5 billion by 2024, according to Global Market Insights.

- Strengths and weaknesses: A major benefit of using a cloud-based firewall is that multiple sites, including small branch offices, can benefit from the protection it provides without having to route all traffic through a central corporate firewall, or to configure and maintain multiple firewalls at different locations. A cloud-based firewall is also highly scalable, unlike an on-premises firewall, which may need to be replaced if the company grows and bandwidth requirements exceed the capabilities of the existing equipment. The key drawback of a cloud-based firewall is that a service provider is unlikely to know the specific security requirements of its customers on an ongoing basis as well as internal staff would. And once a company switches to a cloud-based firewall, it may lose in-house security skills, which can be hard to replace.

- Vendors: Zscaler, Forcepoint, Fortinet.

Container Firewalls

A container firewall is used to protect and isolate containerized application stacks, workloads and services on a container host. It works in a similar way to a conventional firewall, but it also filters all container traffic within a container environment as well as ingress and egress from the protected containers out to external networks and other non-containerized applications.

- Protection level: Medium. All containers require security to be applied to them, but as a relatively new computing paradigm, they are often not well understood. That means that while some level of firewalling is desirable, other security considerations (such as ensuring that the contents of each container is up to date) are arguably more important.

- Do you need it? Although dedicated container firewalls are available, it is also possible to protect a container using a host firewall via iptables running on the container.

- Strengths and weaknesses: A container firewall is likely to be easier to configure than a host-based firewall running on each container. But in smaller environments it may be unnecessary and hard to justify on a cost basis.

- Vendors: NeuVector, Juniper Networks, Twistlock.

Network Segmentation Firewalls

A network segmentation firewall (also known as an internal network firewall) is used to protect sites, functional areas, departments or other business units by controlling network traffic that flows between them. They are implemented at subnet boundaries. That way a network breach may be contained in one area rather than spreading all over the network. It can also be used to provide added protection to areas of the network that warrant it, such as databases, or R&D units.

- Protection level: Medium. Although a network segmentation firewall may prevent an attacker from moving from part of the network to another, in practice it may only slow down an attacker's progress unless the initial breach is detected quickly.

- Do you need it? Network segmentation firewalls are most useful for very large companies, or companies with network perimeters that are very hard to secure.

- Strengths and weaknesses: If an attacker gains access to the network, then a network segmentation firewall may make it significantly harder for them to access particularly sensitive data. But it can introduce performance and availability issues and may present a single point of failure for some network services.

- Vendors: Fortinet.

Functioning of Packet-filtering Firewalls

When a packet passes through a packet-filtering firewall, its source and destination address, protocol and destination port number are checked. The packet is dropped -- it's not forwarded to its destination -- if it does not comply with the firewall's rule set. For example, if a firewall is configured with a rule to block Telnet access, then the firewall will drop packets destined for Transmission Control Protocol (TCP) port number 23, the port where a Telnet server application would be listening.

Packet filtering firewalls work mainly on the network layer of the OSI reference model, although the transport layer is used to obtain the source and destination port numbers. They examine each packet independently and do not know whether any given packet is part of an existing stream of traffic. Packet-filtering firewalls are effective, but because they process each packet in isolation, they can be vulnerable to IP spoofing attacks and have largely been replaced by stateful inspection firewalls.

Functioning of Stateful Inspection Firewalls

Stateful inspection firewalls -- also known as dynamic packet-filtering firewalls -- maintain a table that keeps track of all open connections. When new packets arrive, the firewall compares information in the packet header to the state table and determines whether it is part of an established connection. If it is part of an existing connection, then the packet is allowed through without further analysis. If the packet doesn't match an existing connection, it is evaluated according to the rule set for new connections.

Stateful inspection firewalls monitor communication packets over a period of time and examine both incoming and outgoing packets. Outgoing packets that are requests for specific types of incoming packets are tracked, and only those incoming packets constituting a proper response are allowed through the firewall. Although stateful inspection firewalls are quite effective, they can be vulnerable to denial-of-service (DoS) attacks.

Functioning of Application Layer and Proxy Firewalls

As attacks against web servers became more common, it became apparent that there was a need for firewalls to protect networks from attacks at the application layer. Packet filtering and stateful inspection firewalls can't distinguish among valid application layer protocol requests, data and malicious traffic encapsulated within apparently valid protocol traffic.

Firewalls that provide application layer filtering can examine the payload of a packet and distinguish among valid requests, data and malicious code disguised as a valid request or data. Since this type of firewall makes a decision based on the payload's content, it gives security engineers more granular control over network traffic and sets rules to permit or deny specific application requests or commands. For example, it can allow or deny a specific incoming Telnet command from a particular user, whereas other firewalls can only control general incoming requests from a particular host.

If this type of firewall could also prevent an attacker from connecting directly to the network, it would be even better. Putting the firewall on a proxy server would make it harder for an attacker to discover where the network actually is and create yet another layer of security.

When there is a proxy firewall in place, both the client and the server are forced to conduct the session through an intermediary -- a proxy server that hosts an application layer firewall. Now, each time an external client requests a connection with an internal server (or vice versa), the client will open a connection with the proxy instead. If the connection meets the criteria in the firewall rule base, the proxy will open a connection to the requested server. Because the firewall is placed in the middle of the logical connection, it can watch traffic for any signs of malicious activity at the application layer.

The key benefit of application layer filtering is the ability to block specific content, such as known malware or certain websites, and recognize when certain applications and protocols, such as Hypertext Transfer Protocol (HTTP), File Transfer Protocol (FTP) and domain name system (DNS), are being misused. Application layer firewall rules can also be used to control the execution of files or the handling of data by specific applications.

The Future of the Firewall

In the early days of the internet, when AT&T's Steven M. Bellovin first used the firewall metaphor, network traffic primarily flowed north south. This simply means that most of the traffic in a data center flowed from client-to-server and server-to-client. In the past few years, however, virtualization and trends such as converged infrastructure have created more east-west traffic, which means that sometimes the largest volume of traffic in a data center is moving from server-to-server. To deal with this change, some enterprise organizations have migrated from the traditional three-layer data center architectures to various forms of leaf-spine architectures.

References

- What-is-network-infrastructure: wisegeek.com, Retrieved 15 July 2018
- How-routers-work-816456: lifewire.com, Retrieved 25 June 2018
- Ethernet-and-network-hubs-816358: lifewire.com, Retrieved 28 April 2018
- Network-switching-tutorial, networking-tutorials: lantronix.com, Retrieved 08 July 2018
- Proxy-servers, internet-technologies: tutorialspoint.com, Retrieved 14 May 2018
- Servers-in-computer-networking-817380: lifewire.com, Retrieved 28 March 2018

## 4

Internet Protocol Suite

The Internet protocol suite refers to a set of communications protocols that is used on computer networks and the Internet. Some of the varied topics covered in this chapter include OSI reference model, TCP/IP model, application layer, transport layer, internet layer, etc. for a detailed understanding of internet protocol suite.

A protocol is a set of rules that govern how systems communicate. For networking they govern how data is transferred from one system to another. A protocol suite is a collection of protocols that are designed to work together.

The internet protocol suite is the computer-networking model, which is commonly known as TCP/IP model, because TCP (Transmission Control Protocol) and IP (Internet Protocol) were the two fundamental protocols included in the internet protocol suite. It is a term used to describe the set of communication protocols developed individually by an IT community, for the purpose of communication over networks.

The term internet protocol suite as a whole consists a set of communication protocols that operate in a network layer. It was originally known as DoD model, because the development of internet protocol suite was funded by DARPA (Defense Advanced Research Projects Agency). TCP/IP model provides end-to-end connectivity by ensuring how data should be packetized, addressed, transmitted, routed and received at the destination point. This comprehensive functionality is organized into four abstracted layers namely Physical layer, Internet Layer, Transport layer, Application Layer, which are used to sort all related protocol issues affecting the transmission of data.

Working of Layers

Higher layers involved in internet protocol suite deal with more abstract data, relying on lower layers of to convert the data into forms that can be physically manipulated for transmission. The physical layer or(network layer), containing communication technologies for a single network segment; the internet layer, is responsible for connecting hosts across independent networks, thereby establishing internetworking; the transport layer is providing host-to-host communication and the application layer is responsible for process-to-process application data exchange.

Protocol Stacks

It is possible to write a single protocol that takes data from one computer application and sends it to an application on another computer- A Single stack Protocol. The problem with this approach is that it very inflexible, as any changes require changing the entire application and protocol software. The approach used in networking is to create layered protocol stacks. Each level of the stack performs a particular function and communicates with the levels above and below it. This layered arrangement is not confined to networking, and how it works is probably best understood if you compare it to real life example.

Lets take an example of a parcel service between two offices.

The task is simple – send parcels between people in each office.

We will divide the task into two distinct processes as follows:

1. Take a package, wrap it and address it.

2. Send it to the destination.

At the receiving end

1. Receive the package.

2. Deliver it to the recipient.

Typically you would have an internal mail man that:

1. Collects the parcels from the senders and takes then to a mail dispatch room.

2. The parcels are placed in a van by the dispatcher and then driven to the remote office.

At the remote office

1. The parcels are received by the dispatcher and placed into a tray for the mail man.

2. The mailman collects the parcels and delivers them to the recipients.

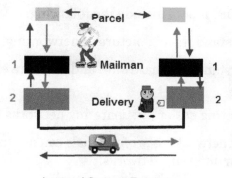

Layered System Example

OSI Reference Model

Most network protocol suites are viewed as structured in layers. This is a result of the Open Systems Interconnect (OSI) Reference Model designed by the International Standards Organization (ISO). The OSI model describes network activities as having a structure of seven layers, each of which has one or more protocols associated with it. The layers represent data transfer operations common to all types of data transfers among cooperating networks.

The protocol layers of the OSI Reference Model are traditionally listed from the top (layer 7) to the bottom (layer 1) up, as shown in the following table.

The Open Systems Interconnect Reference Model

Layer No.	Layer Name	Description
1	Physical	Defines the characteristics of the network hardware
2	Data Link	Handles the transfer of data across the network media
3	Network	Manages data addressing and delivery between networks
4	Transport	Manages the transfer of data and assures that received and transmitted data are identical
5	Session	Manages the connections and terminations between cooperating computers
6	Presentation	Ensures that information is delivered to the receiving machine in a form that it can understand
7	Application	Consists of standard communication services and applications that everyone can use

The operations defined by the OSI model are conceptual and not unique to any particular network protocol suite. For example, the OSI network protocol suite implements all seven layers of the OSI Reference Model. TCP/IP uses some of OSI model layers and combines others. Other network protocols, such as SNA, add an eighth layer.

The main benefits of the OSI model include the following:

- Helps users understand the big picture of networking.

- Helps users understand how hardware and software elements function together.

- Makes troubleshooting easier by separating networks into manageable pieces.

- Defines terms that networking professionals can use to compare basic functional relationships on different networks.

- Helps users understand new technologies as they are developed.

- Aids in interpreting vendor explanations of product functionality.

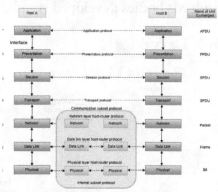

OSI Model and its Layers

Layer 1 – The Physical Layer

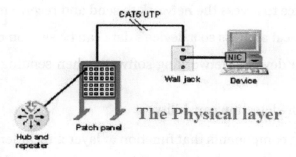

The physical layer of the OSI model defines connector and interface specifications, as well as the medium (cable) requirements. Electrical, mechanical, functional, and procedural specifications are provided for sending a bit stream on a computer network.

Components of the physical layer include:

- Cabling system components
- Adapters that connect media to physical interfaces
- Connector design and pin assignments
- Hub, repeater, and patch panel specifications
- Wireless system components
- Parallel SCSI (Small Computer System Interface)
- Network Interface Card (NIC)

In a LAN environment, Category 5e UTP (Unshielded Twisted Pair) cable is generally used for the physical layer for individual device connections. Fiber optic cabling is often used for the physical layer in a vertical or riser backbone link. The IEEE, EIA/TIA, ANSI, and other similar standards bodies developed standards for this layer.

Layer 2 – The Data Link Layer

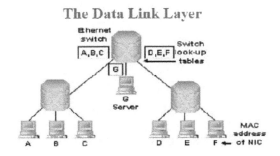

Layer 2 of the OSI model provides the following functions:

- Allows a device to access the network to send and receive messages
- Offers a physical address so a device's data can be sent on the network
- Works with a device's networking software when sending and receiving messages
- Provides error-detection capability

Common networking components that function at layer 2 include:

- Network interface cards
- Ethernet and Token Ring switches

Bridges NICs have a layer 2 or MAC address. A switch uses this address to filter and forward traffic, helping relieve congestion and collisions on a network segment.

Bridges and switches function in a similar fashion; however, bridging is normally a software program on a CPU, while switches use Application-Specific Integrated Circuits (ASICs) to perform the task in dedicated hardware, which is much faster.

Layer 3 – The Network Layer

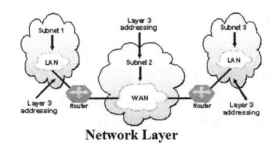

Network Layer

Layer 3, the network layer of the OSI model, provides an end-to-end logical addressing system so that a packet of data can be routed across several layer 2 networks (Ethernet, Token Ring, Frame Relay, etc.). Note that network layer addresses can also be referred to as logical addresses.

Initially, software manufacturers, such as Novell, developed proprietary layer 3 addressing. However, the networking industry has evolved to the point that it requires a common layer 3 addressing system. The Internet Protocol (IP) addresses make networks easier to both set up and connect with one another. The Internet uses IP addressing to provide connectivity to millions of networks around the world.

To make it easier to manage the network and control the flow of packets, many organizations separate their network layer addressing into smaller parts known as subnets. Routers use the network or subnet portion of the IP addressing to route traffic between different networks. Each router must be configured specifically for the networks or subnets that will be connected to its interfaces.

Routers communicate with one another using routing protocols, such as Routing Information Protocol (RIP) and Open version of Shortest Path First (OSPF), to learn of other networks that are present and to calculate the best way to reach each network based on a variety of criteria (such as the path with the fewest routers). Routers and other networked systems make these routing decisions at the network layer.

When passing packets between different networks, it may become necessary to adjust their outbound size to one that is compatible with the layer 2 protocol that is being used. The network layer accomplishes this via a process known as fragmentation. A router's network layer is usually responsible for doing the fragmentation. All reassembly of fragmented packets happens at the network layer of the final destination system.

Two of the additional functions of the network layer are diagnostics and the reporting of logical variations in normal network operation. While the network layer diagnostics may be initiated by any networked system, the system discovering the variation reports it to the original sender of the packet that is found to be outside normal network operation.

The variation reporting exception is content validation calculations. If the calculation done by the receiving system does not match the value sent by the originating system, the receiver discards the related packet with no report to the sender. Retransmission is left to a higher layer's protocol.

Some basic security functionality can also be set up by filtering traffic using layer 3 addressing on routers or other similar devices.

Layer 4 – The Transport Layer

Layer 4, the transport layer of the OSI model, offers end-to-end communication between end devices through a network. Depending on the application, the transport layer either offers reliable, connection-oriented or connectionless, best-effort communications.

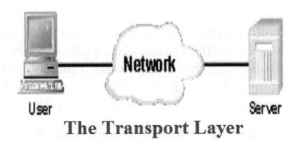

The Transport Layer

Some of the functions offered by the transport layer include:

- Application identification.
- Client-side entity identification.
- Confirmation that the entire message arrived intact.
- Segmentation of data for network transport.
- Control of data flow to prevent memory overruns.
- Establishment and maintenance of both ends of virtual circuits.
- Transmission-error detection.
- Realignment of segmented data in the correct order on the receiving side.
- Multiplexing or sharing of multiple sessions over a single physical link.

The most common transport layer protocols are the connection-oriented TCP Transmission Control Protocol (TCP) and the connectionless UDP User Datagram Protocol (UDP).

Layer 5 – The Session Layer

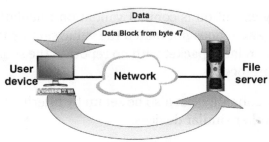

Okay, start the next data at byte 108.

Layer 5, the session layer, provides various services, including tracking the number of bytes that each end of the session has acknowledged receiving from the other end of the session. This session layer allows applications functioning on devices to establish, manage, and terminate a dialog through a network. Session layer functionality includes:

- Virtual connection between application entities
- Synchronization of data flow
- Creation of dialog units
- Connection parameter negotiations
- Partitioning of services into functional groups
- Acknowledgements of data received during a session
- Retransmission of data if it is not received by a device

Layer 6 – The Presentation Layer

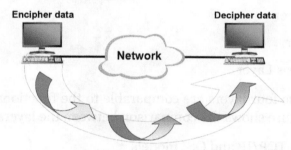

Layer 6, the presentation layer, is responsible for how an application formats the data to be sent out onto the network. The presentation layer basically allows an application to read (or understand) the message. Examples of presentation layer functionality include:

- Encryption and decryption of a message for security
- Compression and expansion of a message so that it travels efficiently
- Graphics formatting
- Content translation
- System-specific translation

Layer 7 – The Application Layer

Layer 7, the application layer, provides an interface for the end user operating a device connected to a network. This layer is what the user sees, in terms of loading an application (such as Web browser or e-mail); that is, this application layer is the data the user views while using these applications. Examples of application layer functionality include:

- Support for file transfers
- Ability to print on a network
- Electronic mail
- Electronic messaging
- Browsing the World Wide Web

TCP/IP Model

The TCP/IP model is a condensed version of the OSI reference model consisting of the following 4 layers:

- Application Layer
- Transport Layer
- Internet Layer
- Network Access Layer

The functions of these four layers are comparable to the functions of the seven layers of the OSI model. Figure shows the comparison between the layers of the two models.

Comparison between TCP/IP and OSI models

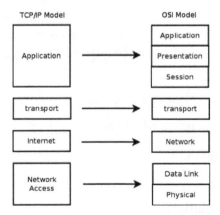

Application Layer

The Application Layer of the TCP/IP Model consists of various protocols that perform all the functions of the OSI model's Application, Presentation and Session layers. This includes interaction with the application, data translation and encoding, dialogue control and communication coordination between systems.

The following are few of the most common Application Layer protocols used today:

Telnet – Telnet is a terminal emulation protocol used to access the recourses of a remote host. A host, called the Telnet server, runs a telnet server application (or daemon in Unix terms) that receives a connection from a remote host called the Telnet client. This connection is presented to the operating system of the telnet server as though it is a terminal connection connected directly (using keyboard and mouse). It is a text-based connection and usually provides access to the command line interface of the host. Remember that the application used by the client is usually named telnet also in most operating systems. You should not confuse the telnet application with the Telnet protocol.

HTTP – The Hypertext Transfer Protocol is foundation of the World Wide Web. It is used to transfer Webpages and such resources from the Web Server or HTTP server to the Web Client or the HTTP client. When you use a web browser such as Internet Explorer or Firefox, you are using a web client. It uses HTTP to transfer web pages that you request from the remote servers.

FTP – File Transfer Protocol is a protocol used for transferring files between two hosts. Just like telnet and HTTP, one host runs the FTP server application (or daemon) and is called the FTP server while the FTP client runs the FTP client application. A client connecting to the FTP server may be required to authenticate before being given access to the file structure. Once authenticated, the client can view directory listings, get and send files, and perform some other file related functions. Just like telnet, the FTP client application available in most operating systems is called ftp. So the protocol and the application should not be confused.

SMTP – Simple Mail Transfer Protocol is used to send e-mails. When you configure an email client to send e-mails you are using SMTP. The mail client acts as a SMTP client here. SMTP is also used between two mails servers to send and receive emails. However the end client does not receive emails using SMTP. The end clients use the POP3 protocol to do that.

TFTP – Trivial File Transfer Protocol is a stripped down version of FTP. Where FTP allows a user to see a directory listing and perform some directory related functions, TFTP only allows sending and receiving of files. It is a small and fast protocol, but it does not support authentication. Because of this inherent security risk, it is not widely used.

DNS – Every host in a network has a logical address called the IP address (discussed later in the chapter). These addresses are a bunch of numbers. When you go to a website such as www.cisco.com you are actually going to a host which has an IP address, but you do not have to remember the IP Address of every WebSite you visit. This is because Domain Name Service (DNS) helps map a name such as www.cisco.com to the IP address of the host where the site resides. This obviously makes it easier to find resources on a network. When you type in the address of a website in your browser, the system first sends out a DNS query to its DNS server to resolve the name to an IP address. Once the name is resolved, a HTTP session is established with the IP Address.

DHCP – As you know, every host requires a logical address such as an IP address to communicate in a network. The host gets this logical address either by manual configuration or by a protocol such as Dynamic Host Configuration Protocol (DHCP). Using DHCP, a host can be provided with an IP address automatically. To understand the importance of DHCP, imagine having to manage 5000 hosts in a network and assigning them IP address manually! Apart from the IP address, a host needs other information such as the address of the DNS server it needs to contact to resolve names, gateways, subnet masks, etc. DHCP can be used to provide all these information along with the IP address.

Transport Layer

The protocols discussed above are few of the protocols available in the Application layer. There are many more protocols available. All of them take the user data and add a header and pass it down to the Transport layer to be sent across the network to the destination. The TCP/IP transport layer's function is same as the OSI layer's transport layer. It is concerned with end-to-end transportation of data and setups up a logical connection between the hosts.

Two protocols available in this layer are Transmission Control Protocol (TCP) and User Datagram Protocol (UDP). TCP is a connection oriented and reliable protocol that uses windowing to control the flow and provides ordered delivery of the data in segments. On the other hand, UDP simply transfers the data without the bells and whistles. Though these two protocols are different in many ways, they perform the same function of transferring data and they use a concept called port numbers to do this.

Port Numbers

A host in a network may send traffic to or receive from multiple hosts at the same time. The system would have no way to know which data belongs to which application. TCP and UDP solve this problem by using port numbers in their header. Common application layer protocols have been assigned port numbers in the range of 1 to 1024. These ports are known as well-known ports. Applications implementing these protocols listen on these port numbers. TCP and UDP on the receiving host know which application to send the data to based on the port numbers received in the headers.

On the source host each TCP or UDP session is assigned a random port number above the range of 1024. So that returning traffic from the destination can be identified as belonging to the originating application. Combination of the IP address, Protocol (TCP or UDP) and the Port number forms a socket at both the receiving and sending hosts. Since each socket is unique, an application can send and receive data to and from multiple hosts. Figure shows two hosts communicating using TCP. Notice that the hosts on the left and right are sending traffic to the host in the center and both of them are sending traffic destined to Port 80, but from different source ports. The host in the center is able to handle both the connections simultaneously because the combination of IP address, Port numbers and Protocols makes each connection different.

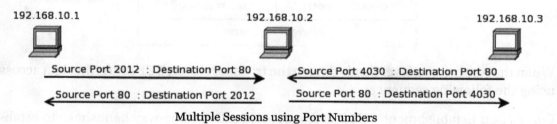

Multiple Sessions using Port Numbers

Table shows the transport layer protocol and port numbers used by different common application layer protocols.

Well-known Port Numbers

Application Protocol	Transport Protocol	Port Number
HTTP	TCP	80
HTTPS	TCP	443
FTP (control)	TCP	21
FTP (data)	TCP	20
SSH	TCP	22
Telnet	TCP	23
DNS	TCP, UDP	53
SMTP	TCP	25
TFTP	UDP	69

Transport Control Protocol (TCP)

TCP is one of the original protocols designed in the TCP/IP suite and hence the name of the model. When the application layer needs to send large amount of data, it sends the data down to the transport layer for TCP or UDP to transport it across the network. TCP first sets up a virtual-circuit between the source and the destination in a process called three-way handshake. Then it breaks down the data into chunks called segments, adds a header to each segment and sends them to the Internet layer.

The TCP header is 20 to 24 bytes in size and the format is shown in Figure Below. It is not necessary to remember all fields or their.

TCP header

Source Port (16 bits)			Destination Port (16 bits)	
Sequence Number (32 bits)				
Acknowledgement Number (32 bits)				
Header (4 bits)	Reserved (6 bits)	Code Bits (6 bits)	Window (16bits)	
Checksum (16bits)			Urgent (16bits)	
Options (0 to 32 bits)				

When the Application layer sends data to the transport layer, TCP sends the data across using the following sequence:

Connection Establishment – TCP uses a process called three-way handshake to establish a connection or virtual-circuit with the destination. The three-way handshake uses the SYN and ACK flags in the Code Bits section of the header. This process is necessary to initialize the sequence and acknowledgement number fields. These fields are important for.

TCP three-way Handshake

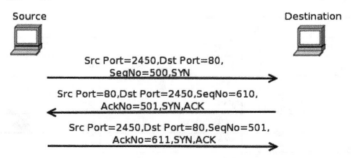

As shown in Figure Above, the source starts the three-way handshake by sending a TCP header to the destination with the SYN flag set. The destination responds back with the SYN and ACK flag sent. Notice in the figure that destination uses the received sequence number plus 1 as the Acknowledgement number. This is because it is assumed that 1 byte of data was contained in the exchange. In the final step, the source responds back with only the ACK bit set. After this, the data flow can commence.

Data Segmentation – The size of data that can be sent across in a single Internet layer PDU is limited by the protocol used in that layer. This limit is called the maximum transmission unit (MTU). The application layer may send data much larger than this limit; hence TCP has to break down the data into smaller chucks called segments. Each segment is limited to the MTU in size. Sequence numbers are used to identify each byte of data. The sequence number in each header signifies the byte number of the first byte in that segment.

Flow Control – The source starts sending data in groups of segments. The Window bit in the header determines the number of segments that can be sent at a time. This is done to avoid overwhelming the destination. At the start of the session the window in small but it increases over time. The destination host can also decrease the window to slow down the flow. Hence the window is called the sliding window. When the source has sent the number of segments allowed by the window, it cannot send any further segments till an acknowledgement is received from the destination. Figure Below shows how the window increases during the session. Notice the Destination host increasing the Window from 1000 to 1100 and then to 1200 when it sends an ACK back to the source.

TCP Sliding Window and Reliable delivery

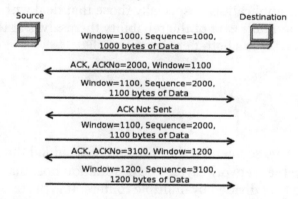

Reliable Delivery with Error recovery – When the destination receives the last segment in the agreed window, it has to send an acknowledgement to the source. It sets the ACK flag in the header and the acknowledgement number is set as the sequence number of the next byte expected. If the destination does not receive a segment, it does not send an acknowledgement back. This tells the source that some segments have been lost and it will retransmit the segments. Figure shows how windowing and acknowledgement is used by TCP. Notice that when source does not receive acknowledgement for the segment with sequence number 2000, it retransmits the data. Once it receives the acknowledgement, it sends the next sequence according to the window size.

Ordered Delivery – TCP transmits data in the order it is received from the application layer and uses sequence number to mark the order. The data may be received at the destination in the wrong order due to network conditions. Thus TCP at the destination orders the data according to the sequence number before sending it to the application layer at its end. This order delivery is part of the benefit of TCP and one of the purposes of the Sequence Number.

Connection Termination – After all data has been transferred, the source initiates a four-way handshake to close the session. To close the session, the FIN and ACK flags are used.

User Datagram Protocol (UDP)

The only thing common between TCP and UDP is that they use port numbers to transport traffic. Unlike TCP, UDP neither establishes a connection nor does it provide reliable delivery. UDP is connectionless and unreliable protocol that delivers data without overheads associated with TCP. The UDP header contains only four parameters (Source port, Destination Port, Length and Checksum) and is 8 bytes in size.

At this stage you might think that TCP is a better protocol than UDP since it is reliable. However you have to consider that networks now are far more stable than when these protocols where conceived. TCP has a higher overhead with a larger header and acknowledgements. The source also holds data till it receives acknowledgement. This creates a delay. Some applications, especially those that deal with voice and video, require fast transport and take care of the reliability themselves at the application layer. Hence in lot of cases UDP is a better choice than TCP.

Internet Layer

Once TCP and UDP have segmented the data and have added their headers, they send the segment down to the Network layer. The destination host may reside in a different network far from the host divided by multiple routers. It is the task of the Internet Layer to ensure that the segment is moved across the networks to the destination network.

The Internet layer of the TCP/IP model corresponds to the Network layer of the OSI reference model in function. It provides logical addressing, path determination and forwarding.

The Internet Protocol (IP) is the most common protocol that provides these services. Also working at this layer are routing protocols, which help routers learn about different networks they can reach and the Internet Control Message Protocol (ICMP) that is used to send error messages across at this layer.

Internet Protocol (IP)

The Internet layer in the TCP/IP model is dominated by IP with other protocols supporting its purpose. Each host in a network and all interfaces of a router have a logical address called the IP address. All hosts in a network are grouped in a single IP address range similar to a street address with each host having a unique address from that range similar to a house or mailbox address. Each network has a different address range and routers that operate on layer 3 connect these different networks.

As IP receives segments from TCP or UDP, it adds a header with source IP address and destination IP address amongst other information. This PDU is called a packet. When a router receives a packet, it looks at the destination address in the header and forwards it towards the destination network. The packet may need to go through multiple routers before it reaches the destination network. Each router it has to go through is called a hop.

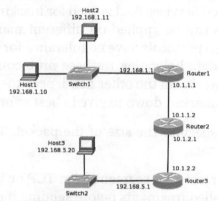

Figure Packet flow in internetwork

Consider the Internetwork shown in Figure Above to understand the routing process better. When Host1 needs to send data to Host2, it does not get routed because the hosts are in the same network range. The Data Link layer takes care of this. Now consider Host1 sending data to Host3. Host1 will recognize that it needs to reach a host in another network and will forward the packet to Router1. Router1 checks the destination address and knows that the destination network is toward Router2 and hence forwards it to Router2. Similarly Router 2 forwards the packet to Router3. Router3 is directly connected to the destination network. Here the data link layer takes care of the delivery to the destination host. The IP address fields in the IP header play a very important role in this process.

Bit 0	4	8		16	19	31
version	Header Length	Differentiated Services (DS) Field			total Length	
Identification				Flags	Fragment Offset	
Time to Live		Protocol		Header Checksum		
Source IP Address						
Destination IP Address						

Figure IPv4 Header

There are various versions of the Internet Protocol. Version 4 is the one used today and version 6 is slowly starting to replace it which is why it's presence has increased on the CCNA Routing & Switching 200-120 exam compared to previous CCNA exam versions. Figure above shows the header structure of IPv4. The following fields make up the header:

Version – IP version number. For IPv4 this value is 4.

Header Length – This specifies the size of the header itself. The minimum size is 20 bytes. The figure does not show the rarely used options field that is of a variable length. Most IPv4 headers are 20 bytes in length.

DS Field – The differentiated Services field is used for marking packets. Different Quality-Of-Service (QoS) levels can be applied on different markings. For example, data belonging to voice and video protocols have no tolerance for delay. The DS field is used to mark packets carrying data belonging to these protocols so that they get priority treatment through the network. On the other hand, peer-to-peer traffic is considered a major problem and can be marked down to give in best effort treatment.

Total Length – This field specifies the size of the packet. This means the size of the header plus the size of the data.

 Identification – When IP receives a segment from TCP or UDP; it may need to break the segment into chucks called fragments before sending it out to the network. Identification fields serves to identify the fragments that make up the original segment. Each fragment of a segment will have the same identification number.

Flags – Used for fragmentation process.

Fragment Offset – This field identifies the fragment number and is used by hosts to reassemble the fragments in the correct order.

Time to Live – The Time to Live (TTL) value is set at the originating host. Each router that the packet passes through reduces the TTL by one. If the TTL reaches 0 before reaching the destination, the packet is dropped. This is done to prevent the packet from moving around the network endlessly.

Protocol – This field identifies the protocol to which the data it is carrying belongs. For example a value of 6 implies that the data contains a TCP segment while a value of 17 signifies a UDP segment. Apart from TCP and UDP there are many protocols whose data can be carried in an IP packet.

Header Checksum – This field is used to check for errors in the header. At each router and at the destination, a cyclic redundancy check performed on the header and the result should match the value stored in this field. If the value does not match, the packet is discarded.

Source IP address – This field stores the IP address of the source of the packet.

Destination IP address – This field stores the IP address of the destination of the packet.

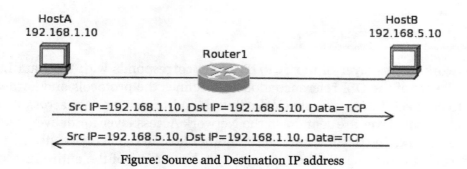

Figure: Source and Destination IP address

Figure above shows how Source and Destination IP address is used in an IP packet. Notice how the source and destination addresses changed during the exchange between Host A and Host B.

Routing Protocols

In Figure Router 1 knew that it needed to send the packet destined to Host3 toward Router 2. Router 2 in turn knew that the packet needed to go toward Router3. To make these decisions, the routers need to build their routing table. This is a table of all networks known by it and all the routers in the internetwork. The table also lists the next router towards the destination network. To build this table dynamically, routers use routing protocols. There are many routing protocols and their sole purpose is to ensure that routers know about all the networks and the best path to any network.

Internet Control Message Protocol (ICMP)

ICMP is essentially a management protocol and messaging service for IP. Whenever IP encounters an error, it sends ICMP data as an IP packet. Some of the reasons why an ICMP message can be generated are:

Destination Network Unreachable – If a packet cannot be routed to the network in which the destination address resides, the router will drop the packet and generate an ICMP message back to the source informing that the destination network is unreachable.

Time Exceeded – If the TTL of a packet expiries (reduces to zero), the router will drop it and generate an ICMP message back to the source informing it that the time exceeded and the packet could not be delivered.

Echo Reply – ICMP can be used to check network connectivity. Popular utility called Ping is used to send Echo Requests to a destination. In reply to the request, the destination will send back an Echo reply back to the source. Successful receipt of Echo reply shows that the destination host is available and reachable from the source.

Network Access Layer

The Network Access layer of the TCP/IP model corresponds with the Data Link and Physical layers of the OSI reference model. It defines the protocols and hardware required to connect a host to a physical network and to deliver data across it. Packets from the Internet layer are sent down the Network Access layer for delivery within the physical network. The destination can be another host in the network, itself, or a router for further forwarding. So the Internet layer has a view of the entire Internetwork whereas the Network Access layer is limited to the physical layer boundary that is often defined by a layer 3 device such as a router.

The Network Access layer consists of a large number of protocols. When the physical network is a LAN, Ethernet at its many variations are the most common protocols used. On the other hand when the physical network is a WAN, protocols such as the Point-to-Point Protocol (PPP) and Frame Relay are common.

Network Access layer uses a physical address to identify hosts and to deliver data.

The Network Access layer PDU is called a frame. It contains the IP packet as well as a protocol header and trailer from this layer.

The Network Access layer header and trailer are only relevant in the physical network. When a router receives a frame, it strips of the header and trailer and adds a new header and trailer before sending it out the next physical network towards the destination.

## 5

Domain Name System

The Domain Name System, or the DNS, is a centralized naming system for entities like computers, services, etc. that are connected to a private network or to the Internet. Some of the significant aspects of DNS, such as dynamic DNS, extension mechanisms for DNS, DNS blocking, DNS hijacking, reverse DNS lookup, etc. have been covered for an extensive understanding.

The Domain Name System (DNS) is a distributed directory that resolves human-readable hostnames, such as www.dyn.com, into machine-readable IP addresses like 50.16.85.103. DNS is also a directory of crucial information about domain names, such as email servers (MX records) and sending verification (DKIM, SPF, DMARC), TXT record verification of domain ownership, and even SSH fingerprints (SSHFP).

Intelligent DNS services can manipulate DNS responses, deciding which IP(s) are returned to ensure the best performance and reliability for clients.

Importance of DNS

DNS is like a phone book for the internet. If you know a person's name but don't know their telephone number, you can simply look it up in a phone book. DNS provides this same service to the internet.

When you visit https://dyn.com in a browser, your computer uses DNS to retrieve the website's IP address of 50.16.85.103. Without DNS, you would only be able to visit our website (or any website) by visiting its IP address directly, such as http://50.16.85.103.

Working of DNS

When you visit a domain such as dyn.com, your computer follows a series of steps to turn the human-readable web address into a machine-readable IP address. This happens every time you use a domain name, whether you are viewing websites, sending email or listening to internet radio stations such as Pandora.

This image provides a high-level overview of how DNS works:

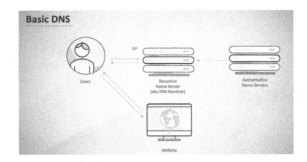

Let's take an in-depth look at the process:

Step 1: Request information

The process begins when you ask your computer to resolve a hostname, such as visiting https://dyn.com. The first place your computer looks for the corresponding IP address is its local DNS cache, which stores information that your computer has recently retrieved.

If your computer doesn't already know the answer, it needs to perform a DNS query to find out.

Step 2: Ask the recursive DNS servers

If the information is not stored locally, your computer queries (contacts) the recursive DNS servers (resolvers) from your internet service provider (ISP). These specialized computers perform the legwork of a DNS query on your behalf. Resolvers have their own caches, and given that many of the ISP's customers are using the same resolvers, there is a reasonable chance that popular domains will already be cached. If this is the case for our example, dyn.com, the process usually ends here and the information is returned to the user.

Just about every ISP runs their own resolvers, yet those aren't necessarily what you could be using. Some companies and perhaps even technically sophisticated home users could run their own resolvers on site. Additionally, there are several very popular open resolvers available, including Google Public DNS, OpenDNS, Dyn Recursive DNS, and Quad9.

Step 3: Ask the root name servers

If the recursive servers don't have the answer, they query the root name servers. A name server is a computer that answers questions about domain names, such as IP addresses. These 13 servers act as a kind of telephone switchboard for DNS. They don't know the answer, but they can direct DNS queries to someone that knows where to find it.

Step 4: Ask the TLD name servers

The root name servers will look at the first part of our request, reading from right to left — www.dyn.com — and in our case, direct our query to the top-level domain (TLD) name servers for .com. Each TLD, such as those for .com, .org, and .us, has its own set of name servers, which act like a receptionist for each TLD. These servers don't have the information we need, but they can refer us directly to the servers that do have the information.

Step 5: Ask the authoritative DNS servers

The TLD name servers review the next part of our request — www.dyn.com — and direct our query to the name servers responsible for this specific domain. These authoritative name servers are responsible for knowing all the information about a specific domain, which is stored in DNS records. There are many types of records, which each contain a different kind of information.

In this example, we want to know the IP address for www.dyn.com, so we ask the authoritative name server for the address record (A record). Some authoritative name servers have intelligence that can analyze an incoming DNS query and return a response that is more performant for the user that originated the query.

Step 6: Retrieve the record

The recursive server retrieves the A record for dyn.com from the authoritative name servers and stores the record in its local cache. If anyone else requests the host record for dyn.com, the recursive server will already have the answer and will not need to go through the lookup process again. All records have a time-to-live value, which is like an expiration date. After a while, the recursive server will need to ask for a new copy of the record to make sure the information doesn't become out-of-date.

Step 7: Receive the answer

Armed with the answer, recursive server returns the A record back to your computer. Your computer stores the record in its cache, reads the IP address from the record, then passes this information to your browser. The browser then opens a connection to the webserver and receives the website.

This entire process, from start to finish, takes only milliseconds to complete.

Dynamic DNS

Dynamic DNS is a service that automatically and periodically updates your DNS's A (IPv4) or AAAA (IPv6) records when your IP address changes. These IP changes are made by your Internet provider.

Functioning of Dynamic DNS

The Dynamic DNS monitors the IP address for changes. When the address changes (which it will if you have a dynamic IP address), the DDNS (or DynDNS) service updates your new IP address.

Significance of Dynamic DNS

It can be very useful for people who want to host their website, access CCTV cameras, VPN, app or game server from their home computer. It is cheaper than to have a static public IP and by setting up Dynamic DNS, you will avoid the need to update all of your records whenever your IP changes manually. Also, static IP address is not always an option; it depends on your Internet provider.

Dynamic DNS is a very flexible option. The way that Dynamic DNS gives a connected device the ability to notify DNS servers to automatically update, alongside the active DNS configuration, IP addresses, configured hostnames and some other information. This saves the need of administrator who should do the changes.

Benefits of Dynamic DNS

DDNS is a very convenient solution, and it has different advantages, but the main ones are the following:

Accessibility – You will be able to access your website or server, easily, without being worried. The IP will change, but this won't stop any of your activities.

Practicality – You don't need a network administrator who to check and reconfigure your settings.

Economic – DDNS makes it cheaper; you won't have IP address conflict in case you have many addresses, and they are used at the same time.

Extension Mechanisms for DNS

The resolver can use UDP protocols to more efficiently obtain resource information when it uses the Extension Mechanisms for DNS (EDNS0) standards. Before these standards existed, UDP responses from a name server were limited to 512 bytes. If a large number of resource records appear on a DNS response message, more than 512 bytes might be required to return all the response data to the resolver. IPv6 resource records are larger than IPv4 resource records, so fewer IPv6 resource records are needed to reach the 512 byte limitation, but the limitation can be reached even with just IPv4 resource records. EDNS0 support permits the resolver to accept DNS messages, using UDP protocols, of greater than 512 bytes, if the name server that is providing the response message also supports EDNS0.

- If the name server does not support EDNS0, these larger responses are truncated to fit within 512 bytes of UDP packet data, and the resolver resends the request using TCP protocols to acquire the entire response message.

- If the name server does support EDNS0, the resolver accepts up to 3072 bytes of DNS response message data in a single UDP packet.

You do not need to configure support for EDNS0 standards. If the resolver is not certain of the EDNS0 capability of a name server, the resolver does not use EDNS0 for that name server and does not indicate on any query that it sends to the name server that it supports EDNS0 processing. After the resolver dynamically determines that a name server supports EDNS0 processing, the resolver modifies the DNS requests that are sent to the name server to use EDNS0.

The resolver dynamically attempts to determine the EDNS0 capabilities of a name server the first time that the resolver receives a truncated UDP response from the name server; the resolver sends the same query to the name server and includes an indication that it supports EDNS0 processing, which is called an EDNS0 probe. The resolver determines whether the name server supports EDNS0 based on the following possible results from the EDNS0 probe:

- If the name server response to the EDNS0 probe indicates that the name server also supports EDNS0, the resolver uses EDNS0 on all subsequent queries to that name server.

- If the name server response to the EDNS0 probe indicates that the name server does not support EDNS0, the resolver does not use EDNS0 on subsequent queries to that name server.

- If the resolver does not receive a response before the timeout period expires, it does not use EDNS0 on subsequent queries to that name server.

No response can indicate any of the following conditions:

- The RESOLVERTIMEOUT value was too small for the larger UDP packet to be received in time.

- The name server ignored the EDNS0 probe query.

- A network router along the path from the name server to the resolver is discarding UDP packets greater than 512 bytes even though the name server and the resolver both support EDNS0.

Because the resolver cannot determine why a timeout occurs, it does not use EDNS0 to that name server for a minimum five-minute interval. At the end of that interval, if appropriate, the resolver sends another EDNS0 probe query to determine whether the name server now supports EDNS0. To fully gain EDNS0 performance benefits, you should choose a resolver timeout value that is long enough to allow larger UDP packets to arrive.

The resolver periodically verifies that the name server does not support EDNS0, even if the response to the EDNS0 probe explicitly indicated that the name server does not support EDNS0. The periodic EDNS0 probe processing allows the resolver to dynamically discover that the capabilities of the name server have changed, although the rediscovery period might take some time. You can use the MODIFY RESOLVER, REFRESH command to cause the resolver to rediscover the capabilities of the name servers more quickly.

To verify whether a name server supports EDNS0, use the dig command with the +bufsize= option to force dig to send an OPT RR record on the request. If the name server supports EDNS0, it responds with its own OPT RR record on the response.

If you have upgraded a name server to support EDNS0, you can issue the MODIFY RESOLVER, REFRESH command to force the resolver to dynamically determine name server capability. The resolver can then use EDNS0 support to accept DNS messages of greater than 512 bytes, using the less costly UDP protocol, which results in improved DNS and resolver performance.

DNS Blocking

DNS blocking or filtering is a common method of denying access to certain websites. Let's have a look at how it works.

Each website is hosted on a web server that has a IP address. For example, the IP address for Facebook is 69.63.176.13. If you type those numbers in your web browser, you will arrive at Facebook's website (may not work if your ISP disallows it).

However, IP addresses are not very user friendly. It's easier to remember facebook.com than 69.63.176.13 isn't it? Therefore the inventors of the internet also created a phone book called the Domain Name System, or DNS.

The DNS translates domain names into IP addresses so that you don't have to remember random strings of numbers. Each ISP (e.g. Streamyx, P1, etc.) have their own DNS servers that functions as phone books for their subscribers.

Whenever you type a website address into your browser, your browser first asks the ISP's phone book what the IP address for that website. Once it's figured out the IP address it will then load the website for you.

With DNS blocking, the ISP is simply removing the record for the blocked websites from their phone book. So when you try to load one of the blocked websites, all you get is a blank screen in your browser because it doesn't know what the IP address is.

Choosing What to Block Using DNS

Today's enterprise-level recursive DNS services provide a variety of options for blocking domain names. Here we will explore some categories and their benefits.

1. Top-level domain blacklist. Instead of choosing domain names to block uniquely, you choose to block entire top-level domains such as .XXX (pornography), .BIT (BitTorrent file exchange servers), or .TOR2WEB (TOR proxies). This approach can be extremely beneficial in reducing the risky categories of domain names from being resolved by your enterprise.

2. New domains. Services such as Newly Observed Domains (NOD) can provide quick protection from domain names that were registered recently for malicious purposes. This type of block list can make it difficult for malware authors to create new domains and use domain-generation algorithms to keep their malicious communications untraceable.

3. Response Policy Zone (RPZ) subscription. Instead of building elaborate lists of bad domain names, DNS RPZ can be used for on-demand lookup of domain names through a service provider to obtain either their reputations or their categories and use them to block the domain names.

4. By response or requesting IP/network block. Domain names that resolve a network block that is either in a country or in an untrusted network zone can be blocked entirely. This approach can also be used to block an internal device or network that is requesting access to an Internet-based resource. Using this method, you could restrict entire internal network segments of your organizations from access to external resources. You can also restrict other risky communications, such as DNS rebinding, in which an external domain name pretends to be a local resource.

5. By anomalous data types and answers. Domain name responses to unknown types of requests (non-RFC complaint, not relevant) and nonsensical responses (NULL) can be used to block DNS tunneling and abuse of the DNS protocol to build covert channels. This method is very effective in eliminating bogus communications or covert channel communications attempts using DNS.

Choosing How to Block

DNS blocking is performed for malicious domains at the recursive boundary of the enterprise using three broad name-response categories:

- Nonexistent domain (NXDOMAIN): This method is used to provide a response that the requested domain or the domain entity itself does not exist.

- Domain redirected: In this case, a malicious domain request is redirected to a local resource to quarantine it and provide support for mitigation and recovery.

- Request denied: The server refuses to answer a specific query (Response Code 5: Query Refused) to disrupt anomalous DNS payloads.

In many cases, the NXDOMAIN response is simpler to implement and provides a way to deny requests to malicious domain name resources. However, NXDOMAIN makes it difficult to provide feedback to users who might click on malicious links or attempt to work around the block, not knowing it is a security violation. These three options give you a variety of choices for planning your "jamming" of malicious communications so that you are able not only to limit risk but also to recover devices that are likely infected in your enterprise. For example, choosing domain redirect to quarantine a set of high-risk domains allows you to collect information on your enterprise computers or systems that are infected with malware.

Challenges to DNS Blocking

It is important to note that DNS blocking poses some challenges to the enterprise. Here are a few practices that your organization can use to reduce their impact on your business or mission and bolster your solution by enabling DNS blocking at your perimeter.

1. Whitelist before blacklist. Trusted domain names and domain extensions that should be allowed in your enterprise to ensure critical communications such as VOIP, email, and communication to trusted partners are not negatively impacted by this capability. It is important that you build a whitelist and ensure that it is maintained with clear documentation, tracking, and lifecycle management.

2. Using DNSSEC. DNS Security Extensions (DNSSEC) enables digital signatures of domain names, making them tamper-proof. Digital signatures can be a challenge to implementing DNS blocking because the enterprise's internal resources

may ignore the answer provided by the DNS blocking system. One mitigation technique is to have the DNS blocking system act as an authoritative server for blocked DNSSEC domains. You can pursue this once you have measured the usage of DNSSEC in your enterprise and assessed the need to prevent any bottlenecks that it introduces.

3. Managing the blacklist (volume, lifecycle, private-vs.-public, classified blacklist). DNS blacklists that are locally managed can quickly become unmanageable in size and complexity. In most cases, it is best to partner with a provider who can manage these blacklisted "zones" and provide responses via RPZ on-demand. This reduces the size of the blacklist while providing an on-demand lookup to valid unknown domains. Enterprises should also manage the local blacklist with clear lifecycle activities and ensure that domains are expired and removed from the blacklist. The slew of blacklist providers can also be difficult to assess, but evaluating them for your industry will help you choose the most appropriate blacklist service provider. I recommend that you reserve classified (government) or proprietary (internal threat intelligence) blacklists for the final lookup, after investigating all the other blacklists, to ensure that your critical threat analysis resources are focused on advanced threat actors. This can be compared to tuning multi-loop control systems, where multiple filters are used to fine-tune an effective control loop. In the multi-loop control systems, the filters with broad "summing point" effect are prioritized at the earliest phases.

4. Logging and analysis. DNS queries for an enterprise can be voluminous, ranging from 30,000 to 80,000 cumulative queries per second in a large-scale enterprise. These can be very hard to log for the entire DNS recursive system. However, logging blocked DNS queries and analyzing them are essential for understanding the effectiveness of your DNS blocking capability. Logging and analysis also enables systematic requests from users to whitelist certain domain names. In addition to applying the general best practices for your cyber security tools, DNS blocking logs should maintain minimal information to sufficiently understand (a) what was blocked, (b) when the blocking was triggered, (c) which downstream device or network requested the blocked resource, and (d) what policy was triggered in the blocking event.

Way Forward in DNS Blocking

DNS blocking will continue to play a critical role in the enterprise cyber security capabilities value chain. The higher end capabilities in your enterprise that do complex work like machine-learning will continue to benefit from indicators such as DNS blacklists. Every enterprise should explore its role and its pertinent approach to enable DNS blocking. As your organization matures in DNS blocking, here are a few forward-thinking ideas in this area to explore to ensure that the service does not become stale but dynamically changes to address new challenges in cyber security:

1. Explore options for Internet Service Provider (ISP) or managed services. An ISP-provided or -managed DNS blocking service can be both cost-effective and simple for your enterprise to pursue. But typically you should consider an ISP-managed service only after you have a DNS blocking capability at your enterprise because first you should understand your organization's needs in this area so that you can effectively communicate these as requirements to an external service provider. An upstream ISP that provides DNS blocking as a service may also be exploring the use of various RPZ providers to ensure security of the data communications. An ISP-managed blocking service could be a viable option.

2. Augment your blacklist with timeliness and context. Many blacklist providers do not offer sufficient context or understanding of domains blocked for malicious usage or malicious intent. This context is critical for an organization that is building its own blacklist and protecting against some advanced threat actors. Wherever possible, augment your blacklist with as much context as possible to ensure that you have sufficient information to analyze blocking events and understand specific threats and risks experienced by the enterprise.

3. Move beyond indicators to understand adversarial techniques. Newer modalities in computing provide the ability to analyze data at scale and use patterns to recognize adversarial techniques. Methods such as machine learning and predictive analysis can help glean knowledge from the data obtained using capabilities such as DNS blocking. Once you have matured your capability and have voluminous data, you can apply techniques to enlarge your blacklist to detect malicious usage patterns and expand your blacklist to capture adversarial techniques (like domain-generation algorithms or domain-registration techniques) instead of specific indicators (like domain names).

Techniques used by cyber adversaries continue to evolve, using more application layer attacks backed by a very sophisticated set of tools. It is necessary for an enterprise defense strategy to be timely, cost-effective, and active to continue to protect its systems and data. DNS blocking is clearly one such capability to activate and mitigate the risks associated with cyber threats.

DNS Hijacking

DNS hijacking is a type of malicious attack in which an individual redirects queries to a domain name server (DNS), by overriding a computer's TCP/IP settings. This can be achieved through the use of malicious software or by modifying a server's settings. Once the individual or individuals performing the DNS hijacking have control of the DNS, they can use it to direct traffic to different websites.

There are actually two main types of DNS hijacking:

1. The DNS hijacking that involves infecting computers with malware or DNS trojan attack softwares, which determines computers to no longer translate the user-friendly domain names to the correct corresponding IP addresses.

2. The DNS hijacking that involves hacking certain websites and literally having their DNS addresses changed so that visitors from these websites end up visiting completely different destinations online.

Functioning of DNS Hijacking

Now that you understand what is DNS hijacking, it's time to learn a little about how it works.

The DNS maps the user-friendly domain name (such as google.com) to its corresponding IP address. DNS servers are usually owned by ISPs and other private business organizations. In normal conditions, your computer is set up in such a manner that it will know to use the DNS from your ISP or other reputable organizations.

If your computer has been infected by hackers or malware programs that managed to change your PCs DNS settings, it will no longer have the ability to correctly make the connection between a user friendly domain name and its original IP address. This means that you will be directed to fake versions of certain websites you are trying to visit.

Uses of DNS Hijacking

If you are interested in cyber security and more importantly, in your own online security, it is important to know the reasons behind DNS hijacking so you know what you should expect and how to avoid it.

ISP DNS Hijacking

This technique is used by several ISPs, claiming it is a way to improve user experience. That means that when connected to the internet through certain ISPs, if you type the URL of a website that doesn't exist or is no longer available, instead of seeing an error page in your browser, you will be redirected to a different website. This translates into more revenue for the ISP, since it is very likely that they control the pages you are being redirected to and earn quite a lot of money from advertising on that site.

DNS hijacking for Pharming

This is done by redirecting a website's traffic to a fake one. As an example, we can take a scenario in which the user is trying to connect to a social networking platform by typing the URL in the browser and instead of accessing the platform, another website appears.

One that is filled with pop-ups and ads and through which the hacker generates revenue from ads impressions or clicks.

DNS Redirect for Phishing

This is a DNS hijack in which the user is directed to a malicious copy of a famous website, which looks exactly the same as the original one. As an example, if a bank's website would be hacked and had its DNS redirected, it would mean that users would end up introducing their log in information on a fake website, owned by somebody who will use their bank information to steal their funds.

Affects of DNS Redirect on users

There are many ways in which you could be affected by this hacking technique and while some of them seem pretty harmless, others are quite scary.

First off, in case you are a victim of ISP DNS redirecting, there is a chance you will not even notice it. There are some inconveniences that could appear: if the ISP DNS server is temporarily overloaded or simply has a downtime, you will not be able to use the internet. On top of this, through DNS redirecting, your ISP can track every single move you make on the Internet, logging everything you are doing on the Internet. Also, if the ISP does not protect its DNS server accordingly, it can end up being exploited by hackers, which in the end would mean that you will end up on rogue websites where your personal information is at risk.

DNS redirects for Pharming are a lot less risky for the end user, but they can be very annoying. If you constantly end up on different websites than the ones you are trying to visit, you will see a lot of annoying ads and there is a chance you will pick up some kind of malware or virus from one of the malicious websites you keep getting redirected to.

By far the most dangerous are the DNS redirects for Phishing. Getting all your personal information or bank information in the wrong hands can turn out to be complete nightmare. Identity theft is a serious crime, and one that you really don't want to be at the receiving end of. Unsuspectingly entering your sensitive data into a website that is not what it seems is a dangerous and scary thing.

Even though it doesn't really affect you directly in any way, you could become a small wheel in the cybercrime system. Since hackers or even ISPs could redirect your traffic to websites loaded with ads, for which they charge the advertising networks for the impressions, one could argue that your are aiding and abetting a fraud against ad networks.

You could be affected by DNS hijacking if your country's government uses DNS redirecting as a way to mask censorship. In certain countries, the access is not permitted on several websites and some of the governments instructed ISPs to redirect users to "approved websites" when they try to access forbidden ones.

Protection Against DNS Hijacking

It's important to stay protected. Your online privacy and personal details are extremely valuable and you should take all the necessary measures to keep them secure. If you want to protect yourself against cyber threats like DNS hijacking, follow these simple rules:

Be Aware of the Issue

Like with most things, the first step would be to become aware of the issue and to try and find out if you've already been affected by a DNS changer. The easiest way to detect a DNS hijack is to use the ping utility. Try pinging a domain you know for sure doesn't exist and if it resolves, there is a very high chance that you are a victim of DNS hijacking.

Stay Away from Shady Websites

Considering that in many cases, the attacks are carried out through trojan horse or similar malware programs, it is highly recommended to stay away from shady websites in the first place. The viruses are usually served through video or audio codecs, through YouTube downloaders or other similar free online utilities. A great example is the DNS Changer Trojan which was used to hijack over 4 million computers, generating a total profit of 14 million dollars through advertising.

Change your Router Password

Changing your router password constantly also decreases your chances of being hijacked. If a hacker targeted your router and is trying to access it to change the settings, it would be best not to find that it is only protected by the default factory password. On top of this, using a good and constantly updated antivirus program could help as well.

Use a VPN Service

Using a VPN service is also one of the most common and effective ways of protecting yourself against DNS hijacking. A VPN would encrypt all your internet traffic and send it through a virtual tunnel. Since this includes all your DNS/Web traffic, your hijacker will be unable to decipher your traffic, which in the end means that you will not have to deal with any annoying or dangerous redirects. On top of this, you can use a VPN regardless of your location, which means that you can stay protected while you travel or while using less secured Wi-Fi networks.

Reverse DNS Lookup

Reverse DNS (rDNS) lookup is the reverse of the usual "forward DNS lookup" where the DNS is queried for the IP address of a certain hostname. In reverse DNS, the DNS is queried for the hostname of a certain IP address. A reverse DNS lookup returns the hostname of an IP address.

Whenever we navigate to a certain webpage, say google.com, our browser checks for the IP address of that domain name and uses that address to find the correct page.

DNS, Domain Name System, is an address list of computers connected to the internet. If you want to go to Amazon, you'll ask DNS where they are located. Just like you would use an address book in normal life.

Note that an address book only works in a one-dimensional way. It's easy to find the address of John Smith from your address book but if you are given an address, it's pretty hard to find out in your address book who lives there - even if you have their address stored somewhere in your address book.

Reverse DNS lookup (rDNS lookup) is exactly this. It's the act of looking up internet hosts by their IP address. Hence the "reverse" part in the name. It's the opposite or reverse way of using the internet's address book, something your old address book can't even do (try finding out who has the number 955-0455-0922 from a paper address book!)

While the internet overall can seem pretty anarchistic at times, this DNS address book is a stable system that everyone on the internet must agree upon. You can pretty much trust that if DNS says someone is google.com they pretty sure are them (and while this blind trust has led to some significant problems, it's the best system we've got).

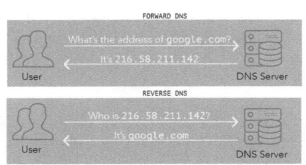

Reverse DNS works the other way around than the usual forward DNS

Now, all internet-connected devices have an IP address. The device you are reading this post has one and the computer that hosts this page has one. If they didn't you couldn't access this page.

While not all, a clear majority of all IP addresses have a reverse DNS record. You can check yours with the tool above. So most computers have an entry of our address book. If we know an IP address, we can know who it is, just like you can see with the tool.

When your browser loaded this page, our server was aware of your IP address and your browser was aware of our IP address, thanks to DNS. This is how the internet works.

Leadfeeder is a tool that shows companies that have shown an interest to your services or products by visiting your website. With Leadfeeder companies can generate new leads every month with reverse DNS.

PTR-record and in Addr Arpa

DNS is defined as zones. Zone is a separate portion of the domain name space and was historically administrated as one zone file. Most often a domain is one zone.

The owner of the zone maps different addresses to different domain names in their zone. For example, maps IP address 23.25.62.12 to point to hostname www in zone example.com. This is done with DNS records.

This would mean that writing www.example.com to would direct our browser to address 23.25.62.12. This is usually done with an A (or ALIAS) record and is the usual forward DNS.

How about reverse DNS? PTR record is the record for reverse DNS. Does the zone owner just add that IP address to their zone and all good? No. Reverse DNS works the other way around.

PTR record is stored in a special zone called .in-addr.arpa. This zone is administrated by whoever owns the block of IP addresses. In our case, the zone for the PTR record would be 12.62.25.23.in-addr.arpa.

The owner of the IP address is usually the ISP and if you want to add a PTR record to your IP address, you need to contact your ISP.

Importance

What this means is that if you have a website, you know all the IP addresses that have visited that website. And with reverse DNS address book we can translate these IP addresses into hostnames.

While most IP addresses can be translated into hostnames, sometimes that hostname is not very useful. Because there's a finite amount of IP addresses and seemingly infinite amount of new mobile phones, laptops and refrigerators connecting to the internet most of the time normal people don't own their addresses. They are merely using an IP address their Internet Service Provider has allocated them for a while.

That's the case usually with mobile phones and home broadband connections. In those cases your hostname will be something like 62-78-145-65.bb.dnainternet.fi. But there's a lot you can still do with this address.

For example, that address tells you that the person is from Helsinki, Finland and their ISP is DNA. You can even pinpoint a more accurate location inside Helsinki where the connection was made from. Nice, but there's still no way you can identify that person with this information.

A simple whois search can reveal more information about an IP address or a hostname

For B2C marketers, this is all you can do with reverse DNS. An IP address can give quite detailed location data and this can help you find good locations to expand your business, for example. But it's all different with B2B marketing.

Most companies have their own IP addresses. This means you can use reverse DNS lookup to see which companies visit your website. In case of a larger company, you can even see from which of their offices the connection was made from.

Using reverse DNS lookup for identifying the visitor is a great B2B marketing tactic. While it can't tell you the name of the person who visited, most of the time just the name of the company can help a great deal (you probably wouldn't want to show your name to every webpage you visit, would you).

Reverse DNS and Email

Reverse DNS is one of the ways email servers use to verify that the sending server is not a malicious spammer. When someone sends email from address john.doe@example.com, the receiving server checks whether the IP address of that server has a reverse DNS record that is tied to example.com.

If the sending email server doesn't have a reverse DNS record at all, that's usually a sign of spam and the email sent from such server is rejected by most email servers.

If you are running your own mail servers, you must have a PTR record set up for your server.

If the email server has a reverse DNS but it's not for your domain, that's not a problem. Just remember that in that case, it's even more important to set up correct DKIM and SPF records.

DNS Record

A DNS record is a database record used to map a URL to an IP address. DNS records are stored in DNS servers and work to help users connect their websites to the outside world. When the URL is entered and searched in the browser, that URL is forwarded to the DNS servers and then directed to the specific Web server. This Web server then serves the queried website outlined in the URL or directs the user to an email server that manages the incoming mail.

The most common record types are A (address), CNAME (canonical name), MX (mail exchange), NS (name server), PTR (pointer), SOA (start of authority) and TXT (text record).

A typical DNS record may look something like this:

```
;   Nameservers
;

    IN   NS   ns1.4servers.com. ;123.456.789.01

    IN   NS   ns2.4servers.com. ;123.456.789.02

;

;   Domain Mail Handlers

;

yourdomain.com.     IN   MX   0  mail

yourdomain.com.     IN   MX  10  mail

;

;

;   hosts in order

;

yourdomain.   IN   A   Your.IP.XXX

www                 IN   A   Your.IP.XXX
```

```
smtp          IN   CNAME   www

pop           IN   CNAME   www

ftp           IN   CNAME   www

mail          IN   A   Your.IP.XXX

;

; end
```

Since DNS records are made up entirely of text, they are easy to modify when needed. However, one small typo could redirect a domain name to the wrong Web server or prevent it from showing up at all. This is why it is important to enter DNS information accurately and double-check your changes entry before saving the zone file.

CNAME Record

CNAME stands for Canonical Name. CNAME records can be used to alias one name to another.

For example, if you have a server where you keep all of your documents online, it might normally be accessed through docs.example.com. You may also want to access it through documents.example.com. One way to make this possible is to add a CNAME record that points documents.example.com to docs.example.com. When someone visits documents.example.com they will see the exact same content as docs.example.com.

Add a CNAME Record

To use CNAME records, select CNAME from the Add Record drop down in the advanced editor. Then enter the hostname you would like to alias from and the fully qualified domain name you would like to alias to. You may also enter @ in the Alias for field to represent the domain itself.

For example, if the domain were example.com and you wanted www.example.com to point to example.com you could put www in the name field and @ in the alias for field.

Error: "Cannot add a new record where a CNAME exists"

To understand the error, it is important to understand that a CNAME points a whole subdomain to another name in the domain name system. If you have another record on that subdomain you can't add a CNAME, as that CNAME would render the other records useless. Let's look at an example:

Let's assume there is an MX record on email.example.com, and now you try to add a CNAME on that exact subdomain (email.example.com). If you added the CNAME, it would override the subdomain (email.example.com) and render the MX record useless, leading to a lot of potential confusion when email stops. To counter this potential confusion, the domain name system does not allow other records alongside a CNAME.

You can achieve a similar behavior as a CNAME with a ALIAS record. Thus, if you want a sub-domain always resolve to the IP address of another domain, you can use a ALIAS record pointing to that domain. You should only do this if you absolutely need it as the ALIAS record does have a small amount of additional overhead when compared to A and CNAME records.

LOC Record

LOC records allow you to specify a physical location for a domain name. It contains Latitude, Longitude and Altitude information as well as host/subnet physical size and location accuracy. This information can be queried by other computers connected to the Internet.

LOC Record Format

A typical LOC record looks like the following in standard BIND format:

$ORIGIN example.com.

@ 3600 IN LOC 31.000 N 106 28 29.000 W 10.00m 1m 10000m 10m

An anatomy of the LOC Record looks like the below:

Name	TTL	Record Class	Record Type	Latitude	Longitude	Altitude	Size	Horizontal Precision	Vertical Precision
example.com.	3600	IN	LOC	31.000 N	106 28 29.000 W	10.00m	1m	10000m	10m

Name

It defines the hostname of a record and whether the hostname will be appended to the label. Fully qualified hostnames terminated by a period will not append the origin.

TTL

The time-to-live in seconds. It specifies how long a resolver is supposed to cache or remember the DNS query before the query expires and a new one needs to be done.

Record Class

Mainly 3 classes of DNS records exist:

- IN (Internet) – default and generally what internet uses.

- CH (Chaosnet) – used for querying DNS server versions.

- HS (Hesiod) – uses DNS functionality to provide access to databases of information that change infrequently.

Record Type

The record format is defined using this field. Common record types are A, AAAA, CNAME, CAA, TXT etc. In the case of a LOC record, the record type is LOC.

- Latitude

- Latitude of the geographical position.

- Longitude

- Longitude of the geographical position.

- Altitude

- Altitude of the geographical position.

- Size

- Diameter of the described location in centimeters.

- Horizontal Precision

- Horizontal precision of the data in centimeters.

- Vertical Precision

- Vertical precision of the data in centimeters.

MX record

MX records or mail exchange records are used by mail servers to determine where to deliver email. MX records should only map to A records (not CNAME records). If an MX record is missing for the domain the mail for the domain will normally be attempted to be delivered to the matching A record. So for the domain "example.com" if there were no MX records for "example.com" then the mail would be attempted to delivered to the apex / root record of "example.com".

Name: This is normally always left blank for MX records. This will be the host for your domain which is actually a computer within your domain. Your domain name is automatically appended to your name. So if you leave it blank it will be the instructions on where to send email for your domain (i.e. username@example.com).

Server: This will be the host (the mail server) that will accept mail for the host that is specified in the name field. Your domain name is automatically appended to your value if it does not end it a dot.

MX Level: The MX level determines the order (which mail server) that your mail will be attempted to be delivered. The mail server with the lowest MX level will first be attempted to have the email delivered.

So if you hade three MX records with levels 10, 20, 30 the following would occur:

Mail would always be first tried to be delivered to the MX record with MX Level of 10. If that mail server is down then the mail will try to be delivered to the mail server at 20. If the mail server at level 20 is down then the mail will be attempted to be delivered at the mail server at level 30. If the mail servers at level 20 and 30 are backup mail servers then the mail will be delivered to the mail server at level 10 when it comes back online. If you have multiple MX records with the same MX level then it will setup a round robin configuration for your email. The sending email server will not send email to both email servers.

TTL: The TTL (Time to Live) is the amount of time your record will stay in cache on systems requesting your record (resolving nameservers, browsers, etc.). The TTL is set in seconds, so 60 is one minute, 1800 is 30 minutes, etc.

Systems that have a static IP should usually have a TTL of 1800 or higher. Systems that have a dynamic IP should usually have a TTL of 1800 of less.

The lower the TTL the more often a client will need to query the name servers for your host's (record's) IP address this will result in higher query traffic for your domain name. Where as a very high TTL can cause downtime when you need to switch your IPs quickly.

Best Practice Tip

If you plan on changing your IP you should set your TTL to a low value a few hours before you make the change. This way you won't have any downtime during the change. Once your IP is changed you can always raise your TTL to a higher value again.

Example – Simple MX record within the same domain:

NAME	TTL	TYPE	DATA	MX LEVEL
mail1.example.com.	1800	A	192.168.1.2	
example.com.	1800	MX	mail1.example.com.	10

Configuration

A record: For the A record configuration explanation please read more in the A – Data Entry page.

MX Record Details

- Name: example.com. is the host which we are making the MX rule for. In the data entry screen we leave the name field blank for the base domain. For most MX record configurations the name is left blank.

- Server: mail1.example.com. is the server that will accept email for example. com. Since the domain name is appended to the end of the server value you just need to enter mail1. If your mail server is in a domain that is outside your domain then you will want to append your FQDN with a dot.

- MX Level: 10

- TTL (time to live): The 1800 indicate how often (in seconds) that this record will exist (will be cached) in other systems.

- The end result of this record is that email for example.com. will go to mail.ex-ample.com which is located at 192.168.1.2. So if you send email to username@ example.com it will be delivered to the email server at the IP 192.168.1.2.

NAPTR Record

NAPTR records are Naming Authority Pointer records defined by RFC 3403. NAPTR records are used for SIP services as part of a mechanism for specifying transport instructions of SIP requests from source to destination which can be sent over a variety of different protocols including: UDP, TCP, or TLS. SRV Records With play a role in SIP services and some implementations use only SRV records.

NAPTR records provide a mapping from a domain to the SRV record containing the instructions for contacting a SIP server with the specific transport protocol in the NAPTR service field, i.e. NAPTR records provide a mechanism for the called domain to specify which protocols it prefers a SIP request to use.

Naptr Record Fields

Field	Description
A) Name	The host name for which the NAPTR record is defined.
B) TTL	The TTL (Time to Live) in seconds is the length of time the record will cache in resolving name servers and web browsers. The longer the TTL, then remote systems will lookup the DNS record less frequently. Your nameservers will also receive less query traffic since most queries are answered by resolving name servers. Conversely, the shorter the TTL the faster any changes you make to your DNS will propagate in servers that have cached data. However, your domain will receive more query traffic. Recommended values: Records that are static and don't change often should have TTL's set between 1800 (being on the low end) to 86400 seconds (30 minutes to 1 day cache). Records configured with Failover or that change often should have TTL's set anywhere from 180 to 600 (3 to 10 minutes cache). If a change is needed for a record with a high TTL, then the TTL can be lowered prior to making the change and then raised back up again after the changes were made.
C) Order	A 16-bit value ranging from 0 to 63535, the lowest number having the highest order. For example, an order of 10 is of more importance (has a higher order value) than an order of 50.
D) Pref	Pref(erence) is used only when two NAPTR records with the same name also have the same order and is used to indicate preference (all other things being equal). A 16-bit value ranging from 0 to 63535, the lowest number having the highest order. For example, an order of 10 is of more importance (has a higher order value) than an order of 50. Since NAPTR records carry additional information, applications may ignore the user preference field in order to find a suitable protocol in the "params" field.
E) Flags	A Flag is a single character from the set A-Z and 0-9, defined to be application specific, such that each application may define a specific use of the flag or which flags are valid. The flag is enclosed in quotes (""). Currently defined values are: U – a terminal condition – the result of the regexp is a valid URI S – a terminal condition – the replace field contains the FQDN of an SRV record. A – a terminal condition – the replace field contains the FQDN of an A or AAAA record. P – a non-terminal condition – the protocol/services part of the params field determines the application specific behavior and subsequent processing is external to the record "" (empty string) – a non-terminal condition to indicate that regexp is empty and the replace field contains the FQDN of a further NAPTR record.
F) Service	Defines the application specific service parameters. The generic format is: protocol+rs. Where "protocol" defines the protocol used by the application and "rs" is the resolution service. There may be 0 or more resolution services each separated by +.

G) Regular Expression	A 16-bit value ranging from 0 to 63535, the lowest number having the highest order. For example, an order of 10 is of more importance (has a higher order value) than an order of 50.
H) Replacement	Pref(erence) is used only when two NAPTR records with the same name also have the same order and is used to indicate preference (all other things being equal).
I) Notes	Add a helpful note with keywords so you can search for your records later.
J) Save	Save your record changes and don't forget to commit your changes after you're done making record changes for this domain.

SOA Record

An SOA (Start of Authority) Record is the most essential part of a Zone file. The SOA record is a way for the Domain Administrator to give out simple information about the domain like, how often it is updated, when it was last updated, when to check back for more info, what is the admins email address and so on. A Zone file can contain only one SOA Record.

A properly optimized and updated SOA record can reduce bandwidth between nameservers, increase the speed of website access and ensure the site is alive even when the primary DNS server is down.

Here is the SOA record. Notice the starting bracket "(". This has to be on the same line, otherwise the record gets broken.

```
;    name            TTL        class     rr        Nameserver
email-address
mydomain.com. 14400    IN    SOA
ns.mynameserver.com. root.ns.mynameserver.com.
(
            2004123001 ; Serial number
            86000 ; Refresh rate in seconds
            7200 ; Update Retry in seconds
            1209600 ; Expiry in seconds
            600 ; minimum in seconds )

mydomain.com.     14400     IN     SOA     ns.mynameserver.com.
root.ns.mynameserver.com.(
```

can also be written as

```
14400 IN SOA ns.mynameserver.com. root.ns.mynameserver.com. (
```

or

```
@ 14400 IN SOA ns.mynameserver.com. root.ns.mynameserver.com. (
```

- Name – mydomain.com is the main name in this zone.

- TTL – 14400 – TTL defines the duration in seconds that the record may be cached by client side programs. If it is set as 0, it indicates that the record should not be cached. The range is defined to be between 0 to 2147483647 (close to 68 years!).

- Class – IN – The class shows the type of record. IN equates to Internet. Other options are all historic. So as long as your DNS is on the Internet or Intranet, you must use IN.

- Nameserver – ns.nameserver.com. – The nameserver is the server, which holds the zone files. It can be either an external server in which case, the entire domain name must be specified followed by a dot. In case it is defined in this zone file, then it can be written as "ns".

- Email address – root.ns.nameserver.com. – This is the email of the domain name administrator. Now, this is really confusing, because people expect an @ to be in an email address. However in this case, email is sent to root@ns.nameserver.com, but written as root.ns.nameserver.com . And yes, remember to put the dot behind the domain name.

- Serial number – 2004123001 – This is a sort of a revision numbering system to show the changes made to the DNS Zone. This number has to increment, whenever any change is made to the Zone file. The standard convention is to use the date of update YYYYMMDDnn, where nn is a revision number in case more than one updates are done in a day. So if the first update done today would be 2005301200 and second update would be 2005301201.

- Refresh – 86000 – This is time (in seconds) when the slave DNS server will refresh from the master. This value represents how often a secondary will poll the primary server to see if the serial number for the zone has increased (so it knows to request a new copy of the data for the zone). It can be written as "23h88M" indicating 23 hours and 88 minutes. If you have a regular Internet server, you can keep it between 6 to 24 hours.

- Retry – 7200 – Now assume that a slave tried to contact the master server and failed to contact it because it was down. The Retry value (time in seconds) will tell it when to get back. This value is not very important and can be a fraction of the refresh value.

- Expiry – 1209600 – This is the time (in seconds) that a slave server will keep a cached zone file as valid, if it can't contact the primary server. If this value were set to say 2 weeks (in seconds), what it means is that a slave would still be able to give out domain information from its cached zone file for 2 weeks, without anyone knowing the difference. The recommended value is between 2 to 4 weeks.

- Minimum – 600 – This is the default time (in seconds) that the slave servers should cache the Zone file. This is the most important time field in the SOA Record. If your DNS information keeps changing, keep it down to a day or less. Otherwise if your DNS record doesn't change regularly, step it up between 1 to 5 days. The benefit of keeping this value high, is that your website speeds increase drastically as a result of reduced lookups. Caching servers around the globe would cache your records and this improves site performance.

Reducing DNS Bandwidth

There is constant bandwidth usage between primary and secondary (backup DNS) servers. This depends a lot on the Refresh value. If the refresh value is say 3 hours, your secondary server is polling your primary server every 3 hours and updating the cache. Lets assume you have a 1000 zone files, each with 3 hours refresh rate. You can imagine the bandwidth that must be getting used. This is especially true if the servers are on 2 separate physical servers.

An increase in the Refresh rate can effectively reduce bandwidth usage between the primary and secondary server.

Increasing Site Speed

The time it takes to access a website on a browser includes the time it takes to look it up on the domain name server. By increasing the "Minimum" value, we're telling the contacting clients to keep their copies of the zone file for a longer time. In effect, reducing the lookups to the nameserver. By reducing the number of times a client has to lookup, we're increasing the site speed.

However, this also means that if you make changes to the DNS record, it will take longer to propagate. If you require to make frequent updates to your DNS records, make sure your Minimum value is lesser than 1 day. That means longer lookup times, but accurate information for the clients

If you are planning a major update on the DNS zone file (say moving to another server or hosting service), reduce the Minimum value a couple of days prior to the change. Then make the change and then jack up the minimum value again. This way the caching clients all over the world will pick up the changes quicker and yet you do not need to sacrifice on site speed thereafter.

Backup Improvement

Always keep a secondary DNS server and keep a higher Expiry value. This will mean that even if the Primary server goes down, the secondary will have the cached copy (for as long as the Expiry value stands) and it will keep serving lookups. Keeping a secondary server but a low expiry value defeats the purpose of a Backup.

Testing of SOA Records

You have set the new SOA values, and you want to know whether the update has taken place. "Dig" is a good tool to troubleshoot and check for DNS information.

For example to check out the SOA records of yahoo.com from all the nameservers, primary and secondary, all you need to do is

```
# dig yahoo.com +nssearch
SOA ns1.yahoo.com. hostmaster.yahoo-inc.com.
 2005122907 3600 300 604800 600 from server ns2.yahoo.com in 0 ms.
SOA ns1.yahoo.com. hostmaster.yahoo-inc.com.
2005122907 3600 300 604800 600 from server ns3.yahoo.com in 0 ms.
SOA ns1.yahoo.com. hostmaster.yahoo-inc.com.
 2005122907 3600 300 604800 600 from server ns1.yahoo.com in 239 ms.
SOA ns1.yahoo.com. hostmaster.yahoo-inc.com.
 2005122907 3600 300 604800 600 from server ns4.yahoo.com in 280 ms.
```

SSHFP Record

Secure Shell fingerprint record or SSHFP Records are DNS records that allow you to publish fingerprints of your servers so they can be verified using DNS lookups when you connect to them. This can be done in a public or using an internal DNS server. Using this method will also stop you from blindly adding machines to your known_hosts file. It's also far quicker than manual verification and checked everytime.

There is lots of software on the internet that allows you to generate SSHFP records however the easiest way is to run the command from the server you wish to validate a connection to making sure you have the public key installed.

To get started login to the server with the key installed and run the command:

```
ssh-keygen -r example.com
```

The records will be produced in the correct format. You don't need to include the shorter hashes as these are sha1. You can now add these hashes to your DNS zone.

To ensure the keys are checked on the client you want to connect from edit the following file:

```
sudo nano /etc/ssh/ssh_config
```

Add the following line as shown below:

```
VerifyHostKeyDNS yes
```

Now connect using the -v command so you see the debug output (leave -i if you don't use a key pair).

```
ssh -v test@example.com -i test
```

You will see in the debug that the keys were found in dns:

```
tom@minty ~                          _ + x
File Edit View Search Terminal Help
debug1: kex: host key algorithm: ecdsa-sha2-nistp256
debug1: kex: server->client cipher: chacha20-poly1305@openssh.com MAC: <implicit
> compression: none
debug1: kex: client->server cipher: chacha20-poly1305@openssh.com MAC: <implicit
> compression: none
debug1: expecting SSH2_MSG_KEX_ECDH_REPLY
debug1: Server host key: ecdsa-sha2-nistp256 SHA256:r4m6K/lsIvkQP/nzoLukp40qoD3t
/pt3doFjufngrVM
debug1: found 4 secure fingerprints in DNS
debug1: matching host key fingerprint found in DNS
debug1: rekey after 134217728 blocks
debug1: SSH2_MSG_NEWKEYS sent
debug1: expecting SSH2_MSG_NEWKEYS
debug1: rekey after 134217728 blocks
debug1: SSH2_MSG_NEWKEYS received
debug1: SSH2_MSG_SERVICE_ACCEPT received
debug1: Authentications that can continue: publickey,keyboard-interactive
debug1: Next authentication method: publickey
debug1: Trying private key: /home/tom/.ssh/id_rsa
debug1: Trying private key: /home/tom/.ssh/id_dsa
debug1: Trying private key: /home/tom/.ssh/id_ecdsa
debug1: Trying private key: /home/tom/.ssh/id_ed25519
debug1: Next authentication method: keyboard-interactive
Password:
```

TXT Record

TXT records hold free form text of any type. A fully qualified domain name may have many TXT records. The most common uses for TXT records are Sender Policy Framework (SPF), DomainKeys (DK), and DomainKeys Identified E-mail (DKIM). TXT records historically have also been used to contain human readable information about a server, network, data center, and other accounting information.

The original specifications for SPF required storage of SPF information for domains within TXT type records. Later specifications created the SPF type record. Currently, there are no SPF implementations that will not use TXT type records if they are present, so SPF type records are not required. There are, however, many SPF implementations that will not use SPF type records, so TXT records remain required. It is a good idea to have identical SPF information within a domain under both a TXT type record and an SPF type record.

- Name: This will be the host for your domain, which is actually a computer within your domain. Your domain name is automatically appended to your name. If you are trying to make a record for the system www.example.com. Then all you enter in the textbox for the name value is www. Note: If you leave the name field blank it will default to be the record for your base domain. The record for your base domain is called the root record or apex record.

- Value: Free form text data of any type. May be no longer than 255 characters. Each word will be treated as a separate string unless one or more strings is enclosed in quotes.

- TTL: The TTL (Time to Live) is the amount of time your record will stay in cache on systems requesting your record (resolving nameservers, browsers, etc.). The TTL is set in seconds, so 60 is one minute, 1800 is 30 minutes, etc. Systems that have a static IP should usually have a TTL of 1800 or higher. Systems that have a dynamic IP should usually have a TTL of 1800 of less. The lower the TTL the more often a client will need to query the name servers for your host's (record's) IP address this will result in higher query traffic for your domain name. Where as a very high TTL can cause downtime when you need to switch your IPs quickly.

References

- What-is-dynamic-dns: cloudns.net, Retrieved 29 April 2018

- Get-around-dns-block-filter: blogjunkie.net, Retrieved 22 March 2018

- What-is-reverse-dns-and-why-you-should-care: leadfeeder.com, Retrieved 12 April 2018

- Dns-record-5349: techopedia.com, Retrieved 30 June 2018

- Understanding-soa-records: bobcares.com, Retrieved 19 July 2018

- Setting-up-sshfp-records: howson.me, Retrieved 29 May 2018

## 6

Internet Exchange Point

An Internet exchange point is the infrastructure that allows the exchange of Internet traffic to content delivery networks and Internet service providers between their networks. Some of the concepts fundamental to the understanding of Internet Exchange Point are commercial Internet exchange and federal Internet exchange, which have been extensively discussed in this chapter.

An Internet exchange point (IxP) is a physical location through which Internet infrastructure companies such as Internet Service Providers (ISPs) and CDNs connect with each other. These locations exist on the "edge" of different networks, and allow network providers to share transit outside their own network. By having a presence inside of an IxP location, companies are able to shorten their path to the transit coming from other participating networks, thereby reducing latency, improving round-trip time, and potentially reducing costs.

Working of an Internet Exchange Point

At its core, an IxP is essentially a data center containing network switches that route traffic between the different member companies that share the costs of maintaining the physical infrastructure. Similar to how costs are accrued when shipping cargo through third-party locations such as via the Panama Canal, when traffic is transferred across different networks, sometimes those networks charge money for the delivery. To avoid these costs and other drawbacks associated with sending their traffic across a third-party network, member companies connect with each other in these special IxP nodes to cut down on costs and shorten distances.

IxPs are large Layer 2 LANs (of the OSI network model) that are built with one or many Ethernet switches interconnected together across one or more physical buildings. An IxP is no different in basic concept to a home network, with the only real difference being scale. IxPs can range from 100s of Megabits/second to many Terabits/second of exchanged traffic. Independent of size, their primary goal is to make sure that many networks' routers are connected together cleanly and efficiently. In comparison, at home someone would normally only have one router and many computers or mobile devices.

Over the last fifteen years, there has been a major expansion in network interconnections, running parallel to the enormous expansion of the global Internet. This expansion includes new data center facilities being developed to house network equipment.

Some of those data centers have attracted massive numbers of networks, in no small part due to the thriving Internet exchange points that operate within them.

Importance of Internet Exchange Points

Without IxPs, traffic going from one network to another would potentially rely on an intermediary network to carry the traffic from source to destination. In some situations there's no problem with doing this: it's how a large portion of international Internet traffic flows, as it's cost prohibitive to maintain direct connections to each-and-every ISP in the world. However, relying on a backbone ISP to carry local traffic can be adverse to performance, sometimes due to the backbone carrier sending data to another network in a completely different city. This situation can lead to what's known as tromboning, where in the worst case, traffic from one city destined to another ISP in the same city can travel vast distances to be exchanged and then return again. A CDN with IxP presence has the advantage of optimizing the path through which data flows within it's network, cutting down on inefficient paths.

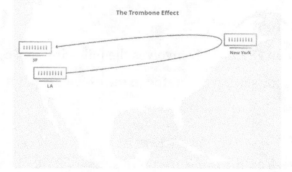

The Trombone Effect

Methods of Traffic Sharing by Providers Across Different Networks

Peering vs paid Transit

The arrangement behind how networks share transit varies. At Internet exchange points, there is sometimes no cost associated with transferring data between member companies. When traffic is transferred for free from one network to the next, the relationship is called settlement-free peering. Unfortunately for many networks, transferring data is not always without cost. For example, large networks with relatively equal market share are more likely to peer with other large networks but may charge transit costs to smaller networks. In a single IxP, member company may have different arrangements with several different members. In instances like this, a company may configure their routing protocols to make sure that they optimize for reduced costs or other conditions by using a protocol called Border Gateway Protocol (BGP).

De-peering

Over time relationships can change, and sometimes networks no longer want to share free transit. When a network decides end their peering arrangement they go through a process called de-peering. De-peering can occur for a variety of reasons such as when one party is benefiting more than the other due to bad traffic ratios, or when a network simply decides to start charging the other party money. This process can be highly political, and a spurned network may intentionally disrupt the traffic of the other party once the peering relationship has been terminated.

Usage of BGP by IxP's

Across an IxP's local network, different providers are able to create one-to-one connections using the BGP protocol. This protocol was created to allow disparate networks to announce their IP addresses to each other plus the IP addresses that they have provided connectivity to downstream (i.e. their customers). Once two networks set up a BGP session, their respective routes are exchanged and traffic can flow directly between them.

The IXP Peering Cost Model

The cost of peering at an IXP usually involves the following cost components:

- Transport fees for getting the traffic to the exchange point

- Colocation fees

- Equipment fees

- Peering port fees on the exchange point shared fabric

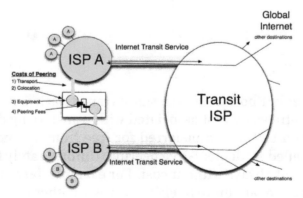

Transport Fees refer to the monthly recurring expenses associated with a physical/data link layer media interconnection into a peering location.

Unlike transit service, transport is not metered; it is sold as a fixed-capacity circuit that costs the same regardless of the amount of traffic exchanged over it.

Colocation Fees are the (typically monthly) expenses associated with operating network equipment in a data center suitable for operating telecommunications equipment.

Not only do colocation facilities provide the operations environment necessary for the equipment, but the better ones also make it easy and cost-effective for their population to interconnect with each other. They understand their customers' businesses and seek to establish and grow a community of participants. A handful of these colocation centers provides much more than space, power, and cross-connects. They facilitate peering.

Equipment Fees are the amortized costs of the networking equipment used for Internet Peering.

Peering Port Fees are the monthly recurring costs associated with peering across a shared peering fabric.

Together, these fees are the monthly cost of peering. These fees are typically the same monthly recurring cost regardless of the amount of traffic that is exchanged over the infrastructure.

For the cost of the interconnection, both parties can then send and receive as much traffic as can fit across the transport circuit and peering fabric.

Establishing the IXP

The hard part with establishing an IXP is not really the technical part, but building a community and trust.

Also, an IXP needs to be sustainable beyond the establishment phase. This includes having enough funds to operate and to upgrade equipment in the future as technology develops and traffic grows. Most IXPs ensure this by setting up a mutual or membership association so that the users of the IXP have equal say in the operation of the IXP. This is by far the most successful model of IXPs today.

The members pay a fee based on their port size to the association, so one fee for a 1GE port and one for a 10GE port. This is not based on the actual traffic, but the port speed. The membership all have one vote each in the running of the organization and normally appoints a board for the day-to-day operation of the IXP.

Secondly, new IXPs tend to believe it is a good idea to offer free ports to large content networks in order to attract other members.

At first glance, this might seem like a good idea, but you will quickly find yourself squeezed between the content networks and the broadband operators, which then also want their ports for free.

Generally, it is better to charge everyone equally and treat everyone equally. It might make it slightly harder for the IXP to get off the ground but it certainly makes running the IXP easier in the long run. Most of the large content owners are also quite supportive of new IXPs being formed in locations or regions where no IXP exists.

Thirdly, what is very important is to ensure that the IXP does not, in any way, interfere with the peering arrangements across the IXP. If the members want to, for example, sell transit to each other across the IXP, that is fine. If someone only wants to peer with a subset of the members, that is also fine.

Selecting the Location for your IXP

Besides creating a community to support your IXP, the other important factor for establishing a successful IXP is its location.

Successful IXPs needs to be accessible for everyone, so it's important to have a neutral data centre where any fibre infrastructure can be built in. These locations can be hard to find but are very critical for success. The wider the choice of fibre providers (or wlan for that matter in some parts of the world), and choice of carriers that are available, the better.

Data centres owned by current or former incumbents are not good choices as they generally tend to be very restrictive in what choice of infrastructure providers they offer.

Besides easy infrastructure access, the data centre also needs to provide a stable power feed, or you need to ensure you have UPSes and perhaps even generators (depending on ambition, the stability of the power grid, and if the data centre provides generator power).

Also, make sure there is room to grow the IXP. You might only start with two racks, but if you are successful you might need more, and moving the IXP is always painful.

Type of Switch Needed

There is an excellent presentation by Remco van Mook that covers many of the same topics as this post, and that also points out that ~50% of IXPs carry less than 20Gbps of traffic. As a new start-up IXP, you will most certainly carry less than 20Gbps.

What you need is a switch that will support 1GE and 10GE ports, preferably via SFPs, not an expensive and large switch with a massive amount of features (although the vendors will try and sell you one).

Instead, make sure you get a switch that you can manage and that you can monitor. These are the most important components of an IXP switch.

Co-location of services

For the benefit of the membership of your IXP, as well as the local Internet community, you should co-locate some critical shared resources with the IXP. The most important ones are:

- The local ccTLD slave service (that is, .uk, .fr, .sg, .bd and so forth). If the ccTLD registry is supportive of the IXP, then contact them and ask if they are willing to locate one of their unicast slaves behind your IXP router. Note: never connect the DNS slaves directly to the IXP L2 domain.

- It is likely that the ccTLD registry also uses an anycast provider for their slave service. In that case, it might be worth contacting that DNS anycast provider and ask them to connect to the IXP. You should, in any case, contact the DNS anycast providers as they are more than happy to peer at many of the IXPs. Many of these also operate or provide service to one of the DNS root servers. These are a critical part of the Internet infrastructure and having one co-located with your IXP will provide a lot of value to your local Internet community. PCH, Verisign and Netnod are some of the DNS anycast providers that locate nodes around the world.

- Route servers are also important to offer to your members, especially as you start to grow. The most stable software for route servers today is BIRD. Providing two route servers also adds redundancy, as if one fails the peering sessions will go down.

- Lastly, some IXPs offer NTP services as part of the IXP to their community. This is a very good service, and something that the community should make use of. However, for a new start-up IXP, NTP services are quite expensive to provide and definitely not needed at the first stage.

Successful IXP

What makes an IXP successful varies.

A small land-locked country where all the ISPs or Internet operators are forced to use satellite capacity for Internet access will benefit enormously from an IXP no matter how little traffic is exchanged, as each bit is a huge saving!

The value of peering is always in the eye of the beholder. Access to one single route or Internet prefix can be extremely valuable to one ISP, while another might need large traffic volumes before it creates value to them.

In the end, a successful IXP is defined by the membership. If there is a community that uses and continues to see benefit from the IXP, they will continue to support it. By being stable and sustainable, the IXP is successful.

Commercial Internet Exchange

In the late 1980s, many TCP/IP networks joined together to form what we now refer to as "the Internet." Besides ARPANET, these groups included the U.S. Department of Defense's MILNET, academia's CSNET, and the National Science Foundation's (NSF) research and educational network, NSFNET. At that point, the Internet was not for ordinary people or businesses. As users moved from the academic Internet into the "real" world—such as graduating from college and accepting their first jobs—they wanted Internet access.

That began to occur with the rise of commercial email systems. In 1989, the little did they know what was to come! Corporation for National Research Initiatives (CNRI) developed an email gateway between NSFNET and the most popular business email system, MCI Mail. The idea of emailing someone across computer networks exploded. Soon, everyone was trying to connect their email systems to the Internet. They used both the eventual standard, the RFC 822 user_name@domain.top-level-domain format we all use now, and a wild mix of other standards, such as UUNET's Bang addressing and X.400. But email was relatively simple.

More important, nobody could charge money for Internet access or allow any kind of commercial activities. The early Internet services dealt with the government, research institutions, or schools, not with individuals. The Internet's acceptable use policies forbade for-profit activities and "extensive use for private or personal business."

IBM, Merit Network, and MCI provided business services over national and regional networks. To save money and expand their reach, in 1990 they formed the nonprofit Advanced Network Services (ANS), which created the first commercial Internet backbone, ANSNET. This same wide-area network was also used by NSFNET, which needed more bandwidth. For the first time, that meant the corporate network and the older Internet were running on the same cables and routers.

ANSNET did more than increase the early Internet's backbone speed from T1's blazingly fast 1.544 megabits per second to T3's then-amazing 44.736 Mbps. In 1993, the NSF also agreed to let the trio of pioneering Internet companies form ANS CO+RE Systems, a for-profit corporation that sold corporate Internet access—as long as they didn't use it for advertising.

This agreement opened Pandora's box. Now, everyone wanted to know how to pay for the rapidly expanding network traffic, as data jumped from business to non-profit networks and back again. To hash out these issues, a public mailing list, compriv, was set up on an early Internet service provider, PSI Network (PSINet). From these conversations, three ISPs that were not part of ANSNET (CERFNET, PSINet, and UUNET), formed their own network of networks: the Commercial Internet Exchange (CIX).

Physically, at first, CIX consisted of a single router that connected their three networks. According to Frank Dzubeck, president of Communications Network Architects, a Washington, D.C., consulting firm, this was the creation of the "backbone of the Internet."

That's because so many other ISPs joined them. In no small part, this was because all the CIX companies agreed to charge each other a flat fee for sharing their network traffic, instead of charging a fee based on how much data was carried.

That was the real beginning of net neutrality, although the phrase wasn't coined until 2003.

However, one ISP, ANS, wouldn't agree to peer—that is, to check traffic with CIX in a net revenue-neutral way. This made it impossible for some groups on one "side" of the Internet to connect with the others.

This troublesome situation continued until 1992, when Mitch Kapor, founder of Lotus Development and its killer-app Lotus 1-2-3 spreadsheet, became chairman of CIX. Kapor got the two sides to agree to a "great compromise." In the agreement, ANS and CIX agreed to share traffic across each other's networks. As Kapor said at the time, "In taking this significant step, we enable greater freedom from content restrictions on the Internet."

With CIX, commerce immediately started flooding the web. And it won't surprise you to know that spam was there from the start. While unsolicited commercial messages began even earlier, in 1994 a pair of Phoenix attorneys launched the first major commercial spam campaign about a Green Card Lottery.

It wasn't until the web came along that e-commerce really started to gain traction. CIX laid the foundation for both great failures, like Pets.com, and great successes, such as Amazon.com.

CIX transformed the collective networks into the Internet you know today: a network in which you can go to any website in the world without worrying about the underlying network.

That's a good thing because while ANS and CIX were working out the network and business kinks to unite the Internet and open it to anyone, Tim Berners-Lee came up with the idea of the web, an Internet-based hypertext system.

Berners-Lee is the individual who took the hypertext idea and turned it into the web reality. He did it not to share LOLCats images, but to help researchers share ideas at CERN, the European Particle Physics Laboratory.

Berners-Lee used NeXT, the BSD Unix-based computers that are the modern-day Mac's most direct ancestor, to create the first web server: info.cern.ch. With the help of Nicola Pellow, a visiting graduate student who created the first web browser, the World Wide Web was off to an inauspicious start in 1991 with the "publishing" of the CERN telephone directory.

It did not make a great first impression. Adoption was slow. It wasn't until 1993 that the first mass-market review of the WEB was written.

The web would have taken off without my help. With CIX and ANS making peace, ISPs sprang up throughout the world, offering Internet access at the unheard speed of 28.8 kilobits per second. The only thing needed now was access to an easy-to-use program that would let users search and play and work with what they found on the Internet.

Enter the Graphic Web Browser.

The first popular graphical web browser was from the National Center for Supercomputing Applications at the University of Illinois at Urbana-Champaign. Mosaic, created by Marc Andreessen and Eric Bina, wasn't the first graphical web browser. ViolaWWW, a Unix browser, takes that honor, and Cello was the first Windows graphical web browser. What Mosaic had going for it was it let you see images within pages. Earlier browsers could only show images as separate files. It was no contest: Mosaic would dominate the first browser war.

It wasn't easy for most people to use the Internet. Windows, the most popular desktop operating system, didn't natively support TCP/IP until Windows 95 appeared. If you wanted TCP/IP on Windows before then, you had to use the notoriously difficult Trumpet Winsock program. (OS/2 had its own web browser built in, which at the time was a real bragging point.)

Still, people loved the idea of the Internet. But none of that—not Facebook, Twitter, Internet memes, Netflix, or World of Warcraft—would exist if it hadn't been for CIX and the web.

CIX made the Internet open, available, and affordable for anyone.

Federal Internet Exchange

A Federal Internet exchange (FIX) refers to two physical locations in the United States that serve as a policy-based peering connection points between U.S. federal government agency networks, such as those used by NASA, the the Department of Energy and the military. There are two FIX points, one on each coast of the United States:

FIX East (FIX-E) in College Park, Maryland, at the University of Maryland

FIX West (FIX-W) in Mountain View, California, at the NASA Ames Research Center

FIX-E and FIX-W are two U.S. based Internet exchanges established in June 1989 by the Federal Engineering Planning Group. U.S. federal agency networks, such as the National Science Foundation Network (NSFNET), NASA Science Network (NSN), Energy Sciences Network (ESnet) and Military Network (MILNET) are interconnected through these FIX points. The existence of these FIX points allowed the ARPANET - a predecessor to today's Internet - to be phased out in the mid-1990s. They are among the hundreds of commercial and community-based Internet exchange points (IXP) established in the U.S. and around the world.

References

- Internet-exchange-point: cloudflare.com, Retrieved 31 March 2018

- What-is-an-Internet-Exchange-Point: drpeering.net, Retrieved 19 July 2018

- Start-internet-exchange-point: apnic.net, Retrieved 26 June 2018

- The-real-history-of-the-modern-internet-1801: hpe.com, Retrieved 16 May 2018

- Federal-internet-exchange-fix-2402: techopedia.com, Retrieved 21 April 2018

## 7

Web Servers

Web server is the server software or the hardware that is dedicated to the delivery of content to the World Wide Web. It involves the processing of network requests over HTTP. An understanding of web servers, hypertext transfer protocol, HTTP header fields and status codes, web cache and security access control methods is required for an understanding of Internet infrastructure. This chapter extensively covers these topics for a detailed understanding.

Web server is a computer where the web content is stored. Basically web server is used to host the web sites but there exists other web servers also such as gaming, storage, FTP, email etc.

Web Server Working

Web server responds to the client request in either of the following two ways:

- Sending the file to the client associated with the requested URL.

- Generating response by invoking a script and communicating with database.

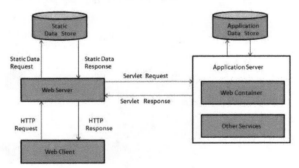

Key Points

- When client sends request for a web page, the web server search for the requested page if requested page is found then it will send it to client with an HTTP response.

- If the requested web page is not found, web servers will the send an HTTP response: Error 404 not found.

- If client has requested for some other resources then the web server will contact to the application server and data store to construct the HTTP response.

Architecture

Web Server Architecture follows the following two approaches:

1. Concurrent Approach.
2. Single-Process-Event-Driven Approach.

Concurrent Approach

Concurrent approach allows the web server to handle multiple client requests at the same time. It can be achieved by following methods:

- Multi-process.
- Multi-threaded.
- Hybrid method.

Multi-processing

In this a single process (parent process) initiates several single-threaded child processes and distribute incoming requests to these child processes. Each of the child processes are responsible for handling single request.

It is the responsibility of parent process to monitor the load and decide if processes should be killed or forked.

Multi-threaded

Unlike Multi-process, it creates multiple single-threaded process.

Hybrid

It is combination of above two approaches. In this approach multiple process are created and each process initiates multiple threads. Each of the threads handles one connection. Using multiple threads in single process results in less load on system resources.

Different Types of Web Servers

In open market there are different types of web servers available. Apache, IIS, Nginx and LiteSpeed are few of them.

Apache Web Server

One of the most popular web server in the world developed by the Apache Software Foundation. Apache is open source software, which supports almost all operating systems including Linux, Unix, Windows, FreeBSD, Mac OS X and more. About 60% of machines run on Apache Web Server.

Customization of apache web server is easy as it contains a modular structure. It is also an open source, which means that you can add your own modules to the server when to require and make modifications that suits your requirements.

It is more stable than any other web servers and is easier to solve administrative issues. It can be install on multiple platforms successfully.

Recent apache releases provide you the feasibility of handling more requests when you compare to its earlier versions.

IIS Web Server

IIS is a Microsoft product. This server has all the features just like apache. But it is not an open source and more over adding personal modules is not easy and modification becomes a little difficult job.

Microsoft developed this product and they maintains, thus it works with all the windows operating system platforms. Also, they provides good customer support if it had any issues.

Nginx Web Server

Another free open source web server is Nginx, it includes IMAP/POP3 proxy server.

Nginx is known for its high performance, stability, simple configuration and low resource usage.

This web server doesn't use threads to handle requests rather a much more scalable event-driven architecture which uses small and predictable amounts of memory under load. It is getting popular in the recent times and it is hosting about 7.5% of all domains worldwide. Most of the webs hosting companies are using this in recent times.

LightSpeed Web Server

LiteSpeed (LSWS) is a high-performance Apache drop-in replacement. LSWS is the 4th most popular web server on the internet and it is a commercial web server.

Upgrading your web server to LiteSpeed will improve performance and lower operating costs.

This is compatible with most common apache features, including mod_rewrite, .htaccess, and mod_security. LSWS can load apache configuration files directly and works as a drop-in replacement apache with most of the hosting control panels. It replaces apache in less than 15 minutes with zero downtime.

Unlike other front-end proxy solutions, LSWS replaces all Apache functions, simplifying use and making the transition from Apache smooth and easy. Most of the hosting companies were using LSWS in recent times.

Hypertext Transfer Protocol

The Hypertext Transfer Protocol (HTTP) is an application-level protocol for distributed, collaborative, hypermedia information systems. This is the foundation for data communication for the World Wide Web (i.e. internet) since 1990. HTTP is a generic and stateless protocol, which can be used for other purposes as well using extensions of its request methods, error codes, and headers.

Basically, HTTP is a TCP/IP based communication protocol, that is used to deliver data (HTML files, image files, query results, etc.) on the World Wide Web. The default port is TCP 80, but other ports can be used as well. It provides a standardized way for computers to communicate with each other. HTTP specification specifies how clients' request data will be constructed and sent to the server, and how the servers respond to these requests.

Basic Features

There are three basic features that make HTTP a simple but powerful protocol:

- HTTP is connectionless: The HTTP client, i.e., a browser initiates an HTTP request and after a request is made, the client disconnects from the server and waits for a response. The server processes the request and re-establishes the connection with the client to send a response back.

- HTTP is media independent: It means, any type of data can be sent by HTTP as long as both the client and the server know how to handle the data content. It is required for the client as well as the server to specify the content type using appropriate MIME-type.

- HTTP is stateless: As mentioned above, HTTP is connectionless and it is a direct result of HTTP being a stateless protocol. The server and client are aware of each other only during a current request. Afterwards, both of them forget about each other. Due to this nature of the protocol, neither the client nor the browser can retain information between different requests across the web pages.

Basic Architecture

The following diagram shows a very basic architecture of a web application and depicts where HTTP sits:

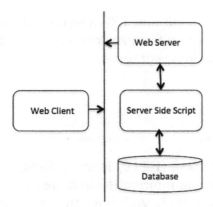

The HTTP protocol is a request/response protocol based on the client/server-based architecture where web browsers, robots and search engines, etc. act like HTTP clients, and the Web server acts as a server.

Client

The HTTP client sends a request to the server in the form of a request method, URI, and protocol version, followed by a MIME-like message containing request modifiers, client information, and possible body content over a TCP/IP connection.

Server

The HTTP server responds with a status line, including the message's protocol version and a success or error code, followed by a MIME-like message containing server information, entity meta information, and possible entity-body content.

HTTP Header Fields

HTTP headers allow the client and the server to pass additional information with the request or the response. An HTTP header consists of its case-insensitive name followed by a colon ':', then by its value (without line breaks). Leading white space before the value is ignored.

Custom proprietary headers can be added using the 'X-' prefix, but this convention was deprecated in June 2012, because of the inconveniences it caused when non-standard fields became standard in RFC 6648; others are listed in an IANA registry, whose original content was defined in RFC 4229. IANA also maintains a registry of proposed new HTTP message headers.

Headers can be grouped according to their contexts:

- General header: Headers applying to both requests and responses but with no relation to the data eventually transmitted in the body.

- Request header: Headers containing more information about the resource to be fetched or about the client itself.

- Response header: Headers with additional information about the response, like its location or about the server itself (name and version etc.).

- Entity header: Headers containing more information about the body of the entity, like its content length or its MIME-type.

Headers can also be grouped according to how proxies handle them:

End-to-end Headers

These headers must be transmitted to the final recipient of the message; that is, the server for a request or the client for a response. Intermediate proxies must retransmit end-to-end headers unmodified and caches must store them.

Hop-by-hop Headers

These headers are meaningful only for a single transport-level connection and must not be retransmitted by proxies or cached. Such headers are: Connection, Keep-Alive, Proxy-Authenticate, Proxy-Authorization, TE, Trailer, Transfer-Encoding and Upgrade. Note that only hop-by-hop headers may be set using the Connection general header.

HTTP Cookie

HTTP cookies, most often just called "cookies," have been around for a while but are still not very well understood. The first problem is a lot of misconceptions, ranging from cookies as spyware or viruses to just plain ignorance over how they work. The second problem is a lack of consistent interfaces to work with cookies. Despite all of the issues surrounding them, cookies are such an important part of web development that, should they disappear without a replacement, many of our favorite web applications would be rendered useless.

One of the biggest issues in the early days of the web was how to manage state. In short, the server had no way of knowing if two requests came from the same browser. The easiest approach, at the time, was to insert some token into the page when it was requested and get that token passed back with the next request. This required either using a form with a hidden field containing the token or to pass the token as part of the URL's query string. Both solutions were intensely manual operations and prone to errors.

Lou Montulli, an employee of Netscape Communications at the time, is credited with applying the concept of "magic cookies" to web communication in 1994. The problem he was attempting to solve was that of the web's first shopping cart, now a mainstay on all shopping sites. His original specification provides basic information about how cookies work, which was formalized in RFC 2109 (the reference for most browser implementations) and eventually evolved into RFC 2965. Montulli would also be granted a United States patent for cookies. Netscape Navigator supported cookies since its first version, and cookies are now supported by all web browsers.

Quite simply, a cookie is a small text file that is stored by a browser on the user's machine. Cookies are plain text; they contain no executable code. A web page or server instructs a browser to store this information and then send it back with each subsequent request based on a set of rules. Web servers can then use this information to identify individual users. Most sites requiring a login will typically set a cookie once your credentials have been verified, and you are then free to navigate to all parts of the site so long as that cookie is present and validated. Once again, the cookie just contains data and isn't harmful in and of itself.

Cooke Creation

A web server specifies a cookie to be stored by sending an HTTP header called Set-Cookie. The format of the Set-Cookie header is a string as follows (parts in square brackets are optional):

```
Set-Cookie: <em>value</em>[; expires=<em>date</em>][; domain=<em>do-
main</em>][; path=<em>path</em>][; secure]
```

The first part of the header, the value, is typically a string in the format name=value. Indeed, the original specification indicates that this is the format to use but browsers do no such validation on cookie values. You can, in fact, specify a string without an equals sign and it will be stored just the same. Still, the most common usage is to specify a cookie value as name=value (and most interfaces support this exclusively).

When a cookie is present, and the optional rules allow, the cookie value is sent to the server with each subsequent request. The cookie value is stored in an HTTP header called Cookie and contains just the cookie value without any of the other options. Such as:

```
Cookie: value
```

The options specified with Set-Cookie are for the browser's use only and aren't retrievable once they have been set. The cookie value is the exact same string that was specified with Set-Cookie; there is no further interpretation or encoding of the value. If there are multiple cookies for the given request, then they are separated by a semicolon and space, such as:

```
Cookie: value1; value2; name1=value1
```

Server-side frameworks typically provide functionality to parse cookies and make their values available programmatically.

Cookie Encoding

There is some confusion over encoding of a cookie value. The commonly held belief is that cookie values must be URL-encoded, but this is a fallacy even though it is the de facto implementation. The original specification indicates that only three types of characters must be encoded: semicolon, comma, and white space. The specification indicates that URL encoding may be used but stops short of requiring it. The RFC makes no mention of encoding whatsoever. Still, almost all implementations perform some sort of URL encoding on cookie values. In the case of name=value formats, the name and value are typically encoded separately while the equals sign is left as is.

The Expires Option

Each of the options after the cookie value are separated by a semicolon and space and each specifies rules about when the cookie should be sent back to the server. The first option is expires, which indicates when the cookie should no longer be sent to the server and therefore may be deleted by the browser. The value for this option is a date in the format Wdy, DD-Mon-YYYY HH:MM:SS GMT such as:

```
Set-Cookie: name=Nicholas; expires=Sat, 02 May 2009 23:38:25 GMT
```

Without the expires option, a cookie has a lifespan of a single session. A session is defined as finished when the browser is shut down, so session cookies exist only while the browser remains open. This is why you'll often see a checkbox when signing into a web application asking if you would like your login information to be saved: if you select yes, then an expires option is attached to the login cookie. If the expires option is set to a date that appears in the past, then the cookie is immediately deleted.

The Domain Option

The next option is domain, which indicates the domain(s) for which the cookie should be sent. By default, domain is set to the host name of the page setting the cookie, so the cookie value is sent whenever a request is made to the same host name. Â For example, the default domain for a cookie set on this site would be www.nczonline.net. The domain option is used to widen the number of domains for which the cookie value will be sent. Sample:

```
Set-Cookie: name=Nicholas; domain=nczonline.net
```

Consider the case of a large network such as Yahoo! that has many sites in the form of name.yahoo.com (e.g., my.yahoo.com, finance.yahoo.com, etc.). A single cookie value can be set for all of these sites by setting the domain option to simply yahoo.com. The browser performs a tail comparison of this value and the host name to which a request is sent (meaning it starts the comparison from the end of the string) and sends the corresponding Cookie header when there's a match.

The value set for the domain option must be part of the host name that is sending the Set-Cookie header. We couldn't, for example, set a cookie on google.com because that would introduce a security issue. Invalid domain options are simply ignored.

The Path Option

Another way to control when the Cookie header will be sent is to specify the path option.

Similar to the domain option, path indicates a URL path that must exist in the requested resource before sending the Cookie header. This comparison is done by comparing the option value character-by-character against the start of the request URL. If the characters match, then the Cookie header is sent. Sample:

```
Set-Cookie: name=Nicholas; path=/blog
```

In this example, the path option would match /blog, /blogroll, etc.; anything that begins with /blog is valid. Note that this comparison is only done once the domain option has been verified. The default value for the path option is the path of the URL that sent the Set-Cookie header.

The Secure Option

The last option is secure. Unlike the other options, this is just a flag and has no additional value specified. A secure cookie will only be sent to the server when a request is made using SSL and the HTTPS protocol. The idea that the contents of the cookie are of high value and could be potentially damaging to transmit as clear text. Sample:

```
Set-Cookie: name=Nicholas; secure
```

In reality, confidential or sensitive information should never be stored or transmitted in cookies, as the entire mechanism is inherently insecure. By default, cookies set over an HTTPS connection are automatically set to be secure.

```
Cookie maintenance and lifecycle
```

Any number of options can be specified for a single cookie, and those options may appear in any order. For example:

```
Set-Cookie: name=Nicholas; domain=nczonline.net; path=/blog
```

This cookie has four identifying characteristics: the cookie name, the domain, the path, and the secure flag. In order to change the value of this cookie in the future, another Set-Cookie header must be sent using the same cookie name, domain, and path. For example:

```
Set-Cookie: name=Greg; domain=nczonline.net; path=/blog
```

This overwrites the original cookie's value with a new one. However, changing even one of these options creates a completely different cookie, such as:

```
Set-Cookie: name=Nicholas; domain=nczonline.net; path=/
```

After returning this header, there are now two cookies with a name of "name". If you were to access a page at www.nczonline.net/blog, the following header would be included in the request:

```
Cookie: name=Greg; name=Nicholas
```

There are two cookies in this header named "name", with the more specific path being returned first. The cookie string is always returned in order from most specific domain-path-secure tuple to least specific. Suppose we're at www.nczonline.net/blog and set another cookie with default settings:

```
Set-Cookie: name=Mike
```

The returned header now becomes:

```
Cookie: name=Mike; name=Greg; name=Nicholas
```

Since the cookie with the value "Mike" uses the hostname (www.nczonline.net) for its domain and the full path (/blog) as its path, it is more specific than the two others.

Using Expiration Dates

When a cookie is created with an expiration date, that expiration date relates to the cookie identified by name-domain-path-secure. In order to change the expiration date of a cookie, you must specify the exact same tuple. When changing a cookie's value, you need not set the expiration date each time because it's not part of the identifying information. Example:

```
Set-Cookie: name=Mike; expires=Sat, 03 May 2025 17:44:22 GMT
```

The expiration date of the cookie has now been set, so the next time we want to change the value of the cookie, we can just use its name:

```
Set-Cookie: name=Matt
```

The expiration date on this cookie hasn't changed, since the identifying characteristics of the cookie are the same. In fact, the expiration date won't change until you manually change it again. That means a session cookie can become a persistent cookie (one that lasts multiple sessions) within the same session but the opposite isn't true. In order to change a persistent cookie to a session cookie, you must delete the persistent cookie by setting its expiration date to a time in the past and then create a session cookie with the same name.

Keep in mind that the expiration date is checked against the system time on the computer that is running the browser. There is no way to verify that the system time is in sync with the server time and so errors may occur when there is a discrepancy between the system time and the server time.

Automatic Cookie Removal

There are a few reasons why a cookie might be automatically removed by the browser:

- Session cookies are removed when the session is over (browser is closed).

- Persistent cookies are removed when the expiration date and time have been reached.

- If the browser's cookie limit is reached, then cookies will be removed to make room for the most recently created cookie.

Cookie management is important to avoid any of these automatic removal cases when they are unintended.

Cookie Restrictions

There are a number of restrictions placed on cookies in order to prevent abuse and protect both the browser and the server from detrimental effects. There are two types of restrictions: number of cookies and total cookie size. The original specification placed a limit of 20 cookies per domain, which was followed by early browsers and continued up through Internet Explorer 7. During one of Microsoft's updates, they increased the cookie limit in IE 7 to 50 cookies. IE 8 has a maximum of 50 cookies per domain as well. Firefox also has a limit of 50 cookies while Opera has a limit of 30 cookies. Safari and Chrome have no limit on the number of cookies per domain.

The maximum size for all cookies sent to the server has remained the same since the original cookie specification: 4 KB. Anything over that limit is truncated and won't be sent to the server.

Subcookies

Due to the cookie number limit, developers have come up with the idea of subcookies to increase the amount of storage available to them. Subcookies are name-value pairs stored within a cookie value and typically have a format similar to the following:

```
name=a=b&c=d&e=f&g=h
```

This approach allows a single cookie to hold multiple name-value combinations without going over the browser's cookie limit. The downside to creating cookies in this format is that custom parsing is needed to extract the values rather than relying on the much simpler cookie format. Some server-side frameworks are beginning to support subcookie storage.

Cookies in JavaScript

You can create, manipulate, and remove cookies in JavaScript by using the document. cookie property. This property acts as the Set-Cookie header when assigned to and as the Cookie header when read from. When creating a cookie, you must use a string that's in the same format that Set-Cookie expects:

```
document.cookie="name=Nicholas; domain=nczonline.net; path=/";
```

Setting the value of document.cookie does not delete all of the cookies stored on the page. It simply creates or modifies the cookie specified in the string. The next time a request is made to the server, these cookies are sent along with any others that were created via Set-Cookie. There is no perceivable difference between these cookies.

To retrieve cookie values in JavaScript, just read from the document.cookie property. The returned string is in the same format as the Cookie header value, so multiple cookies are separated by a semicolon and space. Example:

```
name1=Greg; name2=Nicholas
```

Because of this, you need to parse the cookie string manually to extract actual cookie data. There are numerous resources describing cookie-parsing approaches for JavaScript. It's often easier to use an already-existing JavaScript library, to deal with cookies in JavaScript rather than recreating these algorithms by hand.

The cookies returned by accessing document.cookie follow the same access rules as cookies sent to the server. In order to access cookies via JavaScript, the page must be in the same domain and have the same path and have the same security level as specified by the cookie.

Note: It's not possible to retrieve the options for cookies once they've been set via Java Script, so you'll have no idea what the domain, path, expiration date, or secure flag.

HTTP-Only Cookies

Microsoft introduced a new option for cookies in Internet explorer 6 SP1: HTTP-only cookies. The idea behind HTTP-only cookies is to instruct a browser that a cookie should never be accessible via JavaScript through the document.cookie property. This feature was designed as a security measure to help prevent cross-site scripting (XSS) attacks perpetrated by stealing cookies via JavaScript (I'll discuss security issues with cookies in another post, this one is long enough as it is). Today, Firefox, Opera, and Chrome also support HTTP-only cookies.

To create an HTTP-only cookie, just add an HttpOnly flag to your cookie:

```
Set-Cookie: name=Nicholas; HttpOnly
```

Once this flag is set, there is no access via document.cookie to this cookie. Internet Explorer also goes a step further and doesn't allow access to this header using the getAllResponseHeaders() or getResponseHeader() methods on XMLHttpRequest while other browsers still permit it. Firefox fixed this vulnerability in 3.0.6 though there are still various browser vulnerabilities floating around.

You cannot set HTTP-only cookies from JavaScript, which makes sense since you also can't read them from JavaScript.

HTTP Etag

ETag (entity tag) response header provides a mechanism to cache unchanged resources. Its value is an identifier, which represents a specific version of the resource. Here's an example ETag header:

```
ETag: "version1"
```

Note that value of ETag must be a quoted-string.

Functioning of HTTP Etag

Followings are the general high-level steps where response header 'ETag' along with conditional request header 'If-None-Match' is used to cache the resource copy in the client browser:

1. Server receives a normal HTTP request for a particular resource, say XYZ.

2. The server side prepares the response. The server side logic wants the browser to cache XYZ locally. By default all browsers always cache the resources so no special header in the response is needed.

3. Server includes the header 'ETag' with it's value in the response:

    ```
    ETag: "version1"
    ```

4. Server sends the response with above header, content of XYZ in the body and with the status code 200. The browser renders the resource and at the same time caches the resource copy along with header information.

5. Later the same browser makes another request for the same resource XYZ. with following conditional request header:

    ```
    If-None-Match: "version1"
    ```

6. On receiving the request for XYZ along with 'If-None-Match' header, the server side logic checks whether XYZ needs a new copy of the resource by comparing the current value of the ETag identifier on the server side and the one which is received in the request header.

    ◦   If request's If-None-Match is same as currently generated/assigned value of ETag on the server, then status code 304 (Not Modified) with the empty body is sent back and the browser uses cached copy of XYZ.

    ◦   If request's If-None-Match value doesn't match the currently generated/assigned value of ETag (say "version2") for XYZ then server sends back the new content in the body along with status code 200. The 'ETag' header with the new value is also included in the response. The browser uses the new XYZ and updates its cache with the new data.

Generating ETag Value

ETag specification does not dictate how to generate ETag values. That's entirely up to the application to generate it as it wants. It can be created and updated manually or can be auto generated. Common methods of its auto-generation include using hash of the resource's content or just hash of the last modification timestamp. The generated hash should be collision free. Hash-Collision is the situation when two or more inputs to a hash function give the same output.

ETag Value Validation

Validation of ETag value is nothing but comparing the two values (the one which received in request header 'If-None-match' and the one which is currently representing the resource). There are two validation approaches.

Weak Validation: The two resource representations are semantically equivalent, e.g. some of the content differences are not important from the business logic perspective e.g. current date displayed on the page might not be important for updating the entire resource for it.

The syntax for weak validation:

```
ETag: W/"<etag_value>"
```

Note that this directive is entirely used for the server side logic and has no importance to the client browser.

Strong Validation: The two resource representations are byte-for-byte identical. This is the default one and no special directive is used for it.

HTTP Location

The Location response header indicates the URL to redirect a page to. It only provides a meaning when served with a 3xx (redirection) or 201 (created) status response.

In cases of redirection, the HTTP method used to make the new request to fetch the page pointed to by Location depends of the original method and of the kind of redirection:

- If 303 responses always lead to the use of a GET method, 307(Temporary Redirect) and 308 (Permanent Redirect) don't change the method used in the original request;

- 301 (Permanent Redirect) and 302 (Found) doesn't change the method most of the time, though older user-agents may (so you basically don't know).

- All responses with one of these status codes send a Location header.

In cases of resource creation, it indicates the URL to the newly created resource.

Location and Content-Location are different: Location indicates the target of a redirection (or the URL of a newly created resource), while Content-Location indicates the direct URL to use to access the resource when content negotiation happened, without the need of further content negotiation. Location is a header associated with the response, while Content-Location is associated with the entity returned.

Header type	Response header
Forbidden header name	no

Syntax

Location: `<url>`

Directives

`<url>`

A relative (to the request URL) or absolute URL.

Examples

Location: `/index.html`

HTTP referer

The information that you see written on websites is only a piece of the data that those sites transmit as they travel from a web server to a person's browser and vice versa. There is also a fair amount of data transfer that happens behind the scenes - and if you know how to access that data, you may be able to use it in interesting and useful ways.

The HTTP referer is data that is passed by web browsers to the server to tell you what page the reader was on before they came to this page. This information can be used on your website to provide extra help, create special offers to targeted users, redirect customers to relevant pages and content, or even to block visitors from coming to your site. You can also use scripting languages like JavaScript, PHP, or ASP to read and evaluate referrer information.

Collecting Referer Information with PHP, JavaScript and ASP

So how do you collect this HTTP referer data? Here's some methods you can use:

PHP stores referer information in a system variable called HTTP_REFERER. To display the referer on a PHP page you can write:

```
if(isset($_SERVER['HTTP_REFERER'])) {

  echo $_SERVER['HTTP_REFERER'];
```

}

This checks that the variable has a value and then prints it to the screen. Instead of the echo $_SERVER['HTTP_REFERER']; you would put script lines in place to check for various referers.

JavaScript uses the DOM to read the referer. Just like with PHP, you should check to make sure that the referer has a value. However, if you want to manipulate that value, you should set it to a variable first. Below is how you would display the referer to your page with JavaScript. Note that the DOM uses the alternate spelling of referrer, adding an extra "r" in there:

```
if (document.referrer) {

  var myReferer = document.referrer;

  document.write(myReferer);

}
```

Then you can use the referer in scripts with the variable myReferer.

ASP, like PHP, sets the referer in a system variable. You can then collect that information like this:

```
if (Request.ServerVariables("HTTP_REFERER")) {

  Dim myReferer = Request.ServerVariables("HTTP_REFERER")

Response.Write(myReferer)

}
```

You can use the variable myReferer to adjust your scripts as needed.

Once you have the Referer, what can you do with it?

So getting the data is step 1. How you go about that will depend on your specific site. The next step, of course, is finding ways to use this information.

Once you have the referer data, you can use it to script your sites in a number of ways. One simple thing that you can do is to just post where you think a visitor came from. Admittedly, that is pretty boring, but if you need to run some tests, that may be a good entry point to work with.

What is a more interesting example is when you use the referer to display different information depending upon where they came from. For example, you could do the following:

- General Welcome Message

  ○ You can print the referer URL at the top of your page in a general welcome message. As I mentioned above it's pretty boring, but does offer some basic personalization.

- Welcome Search Engine Visitors

  ○ When someone has arrived at your site from a search engine (i.e. their referer is google.com or bing.com or yahoo.com, etc.), you might want to provide them with a little extra information to encourage them to stay longer on your site. You could point out your newsletter URL or give them links to some of the more popular pages on your site.

- Pass Information to Forms

  ○ If you have a link on your site for people to report problems with the site itself, knowing the referer can be very useful. People will often report problems with a web page without indicating the URL, but you can use the referer information to make a guess about what they are reporting. This script will add the referer to a hidden form field, allowing you some data as to where on the site they may have encountered the problem.

- Create a Special offer for Some Visitors

  ○ Perhaps you want to give people who come from a specific page a special deal on your products or services. This is another example of personalization, where you are shaping their user experience and the content that they see based on their user data, For example, if you sell a variety of products, you can perhaps offer a deal relevant to what they have already been looking at one your site.

- Send Visitors to Another Page

  ○ You can also send people from a specific referer to another page altogether. Be very careful with this, as Google and other search engines might consider this to be misleading and penalize your site.

Block Users with Htaccess by Referer

From a security standpoint, if you are experiencing a lot of referer spam on your site from one particular domain, it can help to simply block that domain from your site. If you're using Apache with mod_rewrite installed, you can block them with a few lines. Add the following to your .htaccess file:

```
RewriteEngine on

# Options +FollowSymlinks
```

```
RewriteCond %{HTTP_REFERER} spammer\.com [NC]
```

```
RewriteRule .* - [F]
```

Remember to change the word spammer\.com to the domain you want to block. Remember to put the \ in front of any periods in the domain.

Don't Rely on the Referer

Remember that it is possible to spoof the referer, so you should never use the referer alone for security. You can use it as an add-on to your other security, but if a page should only be accessed by specific people, then you should set a password on it with htaccess.

X-Forwarded-For

X-Forwarded-For, abbreviated to XFF, is an HTTP request header used to determine the originating IP address of a user connecting to a service through a proxy, load balancer, or CDN. When using services such as a proxy, load balancer or CDN, without XFF, the origin server's logs will display the IP address of the last intermediate service instead of the client themselves. This essentially renders the client's IP anonymous thus making the preventing of abusive activity from a particular IP much harder.

This is where the X-Forwarded-For header comes in as it allows for the IP address of the client to be passed along from the proxy load balancer, or CDN to the server.

Using X-Forwarded-For With a CDN

Taking advantage of the X-Forwarded-For header when using a CDN can also be useful as without it, the IP given to the origin server will be that of the CDN's POP. The client's IP is always displayed as the first one on the left with any subsequent proxy or load balancer IP's thereafter.

```
X-Forwarded-For: client, proxy1, proxy2
```

The example below shows what the request header looks like from a KeyCDN edge server. As can be seen, the X-Forwarded-For header is displayed containing the IP address of the client who requested information. This IP address then gets passed along to the origin server to allow the origin server to be able to identify where the request originated from.

```
GET /foobar.jpg HTTP/1.1
```

```
Host: your_origin_host
```

```
X-Forwarded-Host: <zonename>-<id>.kxcdn.com
```

```
X-Forwarded-For: 178.82.72.134
```

```
X-Forwarded-Scheme: http

X-Pull: KeyCDN Connection: close

Accept: */*

User-Agent: Mozilla/5.0 (Macintosh; Intel Mac OS X 10_9_5) AppleWeb-
Kit/537.36 (KHTML, like Gecko) Chrome/41.0.2272.118 Safari/537.36

Accept-Language: en-US,en;q=0.8,de;q=0.6,ja;q=0.4

Cookie: foobar
```

With the information provided by the XFF header, it allows for certain capabilities that would otherwise be impossible without the end user's IP. Using XFF enables the ability to blacklist certain IPs, redirect particular IP / IP ranges, or even block an end user's IP that surpasses a certain number of requests per second.

The X-Forwarded-For HTTP header is quite valuable as without it, the IP address of the end client is unknown. Being able to identify a particular client's IP is useful for reasons such as stopping abusive activity or simply redirecting particular IPs.

The X-Forwarded-For can be taken advantage of from the origin server or in some cases, a CMS plugin such as in the case of Wordfence.

Do Not Track

Do Not Track (DNT) is an HTTP header field that lets you opt out of third-party tracking by Web sites you don't visit. It may sound straightforward, and it's meant to be just that, but over its short life the situation surrounding the simple standard has become annoyingly complex.

DNT currently accepts three values: 1 signifies the user does not want to be tracked (opt out), 0 means the user consents to being tracked (opt in), and null (no header sent, the default setting) denotes the user has not expressed a preference.

A user agent MUST offer users a minimum of two alternative choices for a Do Not Track preference: unset or DNT: 1. A user agent MAY offer a third alternative choice: DNT:0.

If the user's choice is DNT: 1 or DNT:0, the tracking preference is enabled; otherwise, the tracking preference is not enabled.

A user agent MUST have a default tracking preference of unset (not enabled) unless a specific tracking preference is implied by the user's decision to use that agent. For example, use of a general-purpose browser would not imply a tracking preference when invoked normally as SuperFred, but might imply a preference if invoked as "Super-DoNotTrack" or "UltraPrivacyFred".

Implementations of HTTP that are not under control of the user MUST NOT add, delete, or modify a tracking preference. Some controlled network environments, such as public access terminals or managed corporate intranets, might impose restrictions on the use or configuration of installed user agents, such that a user might only have access to user agents with a predetermined preference enabled. However, if a user brings their own Web-enabled device to a library or cafe with wireless Internet access, the expectation will be that their chosen user agent and personal preferences regarding Web site behavior will not be altered by the network environment (aside from blanket limitations on what resources can or cannot be accessed through that network).

An HTTP intermediary MUST NOT add, delete, or modify a tracking preference expression in a request forwarded through that intermediary unless the intermediary has been specifically installed or configured to do so by the user making the request. For example, an Internet Service Provider MUST NOT injects DNT: 1 on behalf of all users who have not expressed a preference.

User agents often include user-installable extensions, also known as add-ons or plug-ins, that are capable of modifying configurations and making network requests. From the user's perspective, these extensions are considered part of the user agent and ought to respect the user's configuration of a tracking preference. The user agent as a whole is responsible for ensuring conformance with this protocol, to the extent possible, which means the user agent core and each extension are jointly responsible for conformance. However, there is no single standard for extension interfaces. A user agent that permits such extensions SHOULD provide an appropriate mechanism for extensions to determine the user's tracking preference.

A user agent extension MUST NOT alter the tracking preference expression or its associated configuration unless the act of installing and enabling that extension is an explicit choice by the user for that tracking preference, or the extension itself complies with all of the requirements this protocol places on a user agent.

Likewise, software outside of the user agent might filter network traffic or cause a user agent's configuration to be changed. Software that alters a user agent configuration MUST adhere to the above requirements on a user agent extension. Software that filters network traffic MUST adhere to the above requirements on an HTTP intermediary.

Aside from the above requirements, we do not specify how the tracking preference choices are offered to the user or how the preference is enabled: each implementation is responsible for determining the user experience by which a tracking preference is enabled.

For example, a user might select a check-box in their user agent's configuration, install an extension that is specifically designed to add a tracking preference expression, or make a choice for privacy that then implicitly includes a tracking preference (e.g., Privacy settings: high). A user agent might ask the user for their preference during startup, perhaps on first use or after an update adds the tracking protection feature. Likewise, a user might install or configure a proxy to add the expression to their own outgoing requests.

Expressing a Tracking Preference

Expression Format

When a user has enabled a tracking preference, that preference needs to be expressed to all mechanisms that might perform or initiate tracking.

When enabled, a tracking preference is expressed as either:

DNT	Meaning
1	This user prefers not to be tracked on this request.
0	This user prefers to allow tracking on this request.

A user agent MUST NOT send a tracking preference expression if a tracking preference is not enabled. This means that no expression is sent for each of the following cases:

- The user agent does not implement this protocol;

- The user has not yet made a choice for a specific preference; or,

- The user has chosen not to transmit a preference.

In the absence of regulatory, legal, or other requirements, servers MAY interpret the lack of an expressed tracking preference as they find most appropriate for the given user, particularly when considered in light of the user's privacy expectations and cultural circumstances. Likewise, servers might make use of other preference information outside the scope of this protocol, such as site-specific user preferences or third-party registration services, to inform or adjust their behavior when no explicit preference is expressed via this protocol.

DNT Header Field for HTTP Requests

The DNT header field is a mechanism for expressing the user's tracking preference in an HTTP request ([RFC7230]). At most one DNT header field can be present in a valid request.

```
DNT-field-name  = "DNT"

DNT-field-value = ( "0" / "1" ) *DNT-extension
```

A user agent MUST NOT generate a DNT header field if the user's tracking preference is not enabled.

A user agent MUST generate a DNT header field with a field-value that begins with the numeric character "1" if the user's tracking preference is enabled, their preference is for DNT: 1, and no exception has been granted for the target resource.

A user agent MUST generate a DNT header field with a field-value that begins with the numeric character "0" if the user's tracking preference is enabled and their preference is for DNT:0, or if an exception has been granted for the target resource.

A proxy MUST NOT generate a DNT header field unless it has been specifically installed or configured to do so by the user making the request and adheres to the above requirements as if it were a user agent.

EXAMPLE

```
GET /something/here HTTP/1.1

Host: example.com

DNT: 1
```

HTTP Status Codes

HTTP, Hypertext Transfer Protocol, is the method by which clients (i.e. you) and servers communicate. When someone clicks a link, types in a URL or submits out a form, their browser sends a request to a server for information. It might be asking for a page, or sending data, but either way that is called an HTTP Request. When a server receives that request, it sends back an HTTP Response, with information for the client. Usually, this is invisible, though I'm sure you've seen one of the very common Response codes - 404, indicating a page was not found. There are a fair few more status codes sent by servers, and the following is a list of the current ones in HTTP 1.1, along with an explanation of their meanings.

Informational

- 100 - Continue

   A status code of 100 indicates that (usually the first) part of a request has been received without any problems, and that the rest of the request should now be sent.

- 101 - Switching Protocols

   HTTP 1.1 is just one type of protocol for transferring data on the web, and a status code of 101 indicates that the server is changing to the protocol it defines in the "Upgrade" header it returns to the client. For example, when requesting a page, a browser might receive a static code of 101, followed by an "Upgrade" header showing that the server is changing to a different version of HTTP.

Successful

- 200 - OK

  The 200 status code is by far the most common returned. It means, simply, that the request was received and understood and is being processed.

- 201 - Created

  A 201 status code indicates that a request was successful and as a result, a resource has been created (for example a new page).

- 202 - Accepted

  The status code 202 indicates that server has received and understood the request, and that it has been accepted for processing, although it may not be processed immediately.

- 203 - Non-Authoritative Information

  A 203 status code means that the request was received and understood, and that information sent back about the response is from a third party, rather than the original server. This is virtually identical in meaning to a 200 status code.

- 204 - No Content

  The 204 status code means that the request was received and understood, but that there is no need to send any data back.

- 205 - Reset Content

  The 205 status code is a request from the server to the client to reset the document from which the original request was sent. For example, if a user fills out a form, and submits it, a status code of 205 means the server is asking the browser to clear the form.

- 206 - Partial Content

  A status code of 206 is a response to a request for part of a document. This is used by advanced caching tools, when a user agent requests only a small part of a page, and just that section is returned.

Redirection

- 300 - Multiple Choices

  The 300 status code indicates that a resource has moved. The response will also include a list of locations from which the user agent can select the most appropriate.

- 301 - Moved Permanently

  A status code of 301 tells a client that the resource they asked for has permanently moved to a new location. The response should also include this location. It tells the client to use the new URL the next time it wants to fetch the same resource.

- 302 - Found

  A status code of 302 tells a client that the resource they asked for has temporarily moved to a new location. The response should also include this location. It tells the client that it should carry on using the same URL to access this resource.

- 303 - See Other

  A 303 status code indicates that the response to the request can be found at the specified URL, and should be retrieved from there. It does not mean that something has moved - it is simply specifying the address at which the response to the request can be found.

- 304 - Not Modified

  The 304 status code is sent in response to a request (for a document) that asked for the document only if it was newer than the one the client already had. Normally, when a document is cached, the date it was cached is stored. The next time the document is viewed, the client asks the server if the document has changed. If not, the client just reloads the document from the cache.

- 305 - Use Proxy

  A 305 status code tells the client that the requested resource has to be reached through a proxy, which will be specified in the response.

- 307 - Temporary Redirect

  307 is the status code that is sent when a document is temporarily available at a different URL, which is also returned. There is very little difference between a 302 status code and a 307 status code. 307 was created as another, less ambiguous, version of the 302 status code.

Client Error

- 400 - Bad Request

  A status code of 400 indicates that the server did not understand the request due to bad syntax.

- 401 - Unauthorized

  A 401 status code indicates that before a resource can be accessed, the client must be authorised by the server.

- 402 - Payment Required

  The 402 status code is not currently in use, being listed as "reserved for future use".

- 403 - Forbidden

  A 403 status code indicates that the client cannot access the requested resource. That might mean that the wrong username and password were sent in the request, or that the permissions on the server do not allow what was being asked.

- 404 - Not Found

  The best known of them all, the 404 status code indicates that the requested resource was not found at the URL given, and the server has no idea how long for.

- 405 - Method Not Allowed

  A 405 status code is returned when the client has tried to use a request method that the server does not allow. Request methods that are allowed should be sent with the response (common request methods are POST and GET).

- 406 - Not Acceptable

  The 406 status code means that, although the server understood and processed the request, the response is of a form the client cannot understand. A client sends, as part of a request, headers indicating what types of data it can use, and a 406 error is returned when the response is of a type not i that list.

- 407 - Proxy Authentication Required

  The 407 status code is very similar to the 401 status code, and means that the client must be authorised by the proxy before the request can proceed.

- 408 - Request Timeout

  A 408 status code means that the client did not produce a request quickly enough. A server is set to only wait a certain amount of time for responses from clients, and a 408 status code indicates that time has passed.

- 409 - Conflict

A 409 status code indicates that the server was unable to complete the request, often because a file would need to be edited, created or deleted, and that file cannot be edited, created or deleted.

- 410 - Gone

A 410 status code is the 404's lesser known cousin. It indicates that a resource has permanently gone (a 404 status code gives no indication if a resource has gone permanently or temporarily), and no new address is known for it.

- 411 - Length Required

The 411 status code occurs when a server refuses to process a request because a content length was not specified.

- 412 - Precondition Failed

A 412 status code indicates that one of the conditions the request was made under has failed.

- 413 - Request Entity Too Large

The 413 status code indicates that the request was larger than the server is able to handle, either due to physical constraints or to settings. Usually, this occurs when a file is sent using the POST method from a form, and the file is larger than the maximum size allowed in the server settings.

- 414 - Request-URI Too Long

The 414 status code indicates the URL requested by the client was longer than it can process.

- 415 - Unsupported Media Type

A 415 status code is returned by a server to indicate that part of the request was in an unsupported format.

- 416 - Requested Range Not Satisfiable

A 416 status code indicates that the server was unable to fulfill the request. This may be, for example, because the client asked for the 800th-900th bytes of a document, but the document was only 200 bytes long.

- 417 - Expectation Failed

The 417 status code means that the server was unable to properly complete the request. One of the headers sent to the server, the "Expect" header, indicated an expectation the server could not meet.

Server Error

- 500 - Internal Server Error

  A 500 status code (all too often seen by Perl programmers) indicates that the server encountered something it didn't expect and was unable to complete the request.

- 501 - Not Implemented

  The 501 status code indicates that the server does not support all that is needed for the request to be completed.

- 502 - Bad Gateway

  A 502 status code indicates that a server, while acting as a proxy, received a response from a server further upstream that it judged invalid.

- 503 - Service Unavailable

  A 503 status code is most often seen on extremely busy servers, and it indicates that the server was unable to complete the request due to a server overload.

- 504 - Gateway Timeout

  A 504 status code is returned when a server acting as a proxy has waited too long for a response from a server further upstream.

- 505 - HTTP Version Not Supported

  A 505 status code is returned when the HTTP version indicated in the request is no supported. The response should indicate which HTTP versions are supported.

Security Access Control Methods

Access control is a security technique that regulates who or what can view or use resources in a computing environment. It is a fundamental concept in security that minimizes risk to the business or organization.

There are two types of access control: physical and logical. Physical access control limits access to campuses, buildings, rooms and physical IT assets. Logical access control limits connections to computer networks, system files and data.

To secure a facility, organizations use electronic access control systems that rely on user credentials, access card readers, auditing and reports to track employee access to restricted business locations and proprietary areas, such as data centers. Some of these systems incorporate access control panels to restrict entry to rooms and buildings as well as alarms and lockdown capabilities to prevent unauthorized access or operations.

Access control systems perform identification authentication and authorization of users and entities by evaluating required login credentials that can include passwords, personal identification numbers (PINs), biometric scans, security tokens or other authentication factors. Multifactor authentication, which requires two or more authentication factors, is often an important part of layered defense to protect access control systems.

These security controls work by identifying an individual or entity, verifying that the person or application is who or what it claims to be, and authorizing the access level and set of actions associated with the username or IP address. Directory services and protocols, including the Local Directory Access Protocol (LDAP) and the Security Assertion Markup Language (SAML), provide access controls for authenticating and authorizing users and entities and enabling them to connect to computer resources, such as distributed applications and web servers.

Organizations use different access control models depending on their compliance requirements and the security levels of information technology they are trying to protect.

Types of Access Control

The main types of access control are:

- Mandatory access control (MAC): A security model in which access rights are regulated by a central authority based on multiple levels of security. Often used in government and military environments, classifications are assigned to system resources and the operating system or security kernel, grants or denies access to those resource objects based on the information security clearance of the user or device. For example, Security Enhanced Linux is an implementation of MAC on the Linux operating system.

- Discretionary access control (DAC): An access control method in which owners or administrators of the protected system, data or resource set the policies defining who or what is authorized to access the resource. Many of these systems enable administrators to limit the propagation of access rights. A common criticism of DAC systems is a lack of centralized control.

- Role-based access control (RBAC): A widely used access control mechanism that restricts access to computer resources based on individuals or groups with defined business functions -- executive level, engineer level 1 -- rather than the identities of individual users. The role-based security model relies on a complex structure of role assignments; role authorizations and role permissions developed using role engineering to regulate employee access to systems. RBAC systems can be used to enforce MAC and DAC frameworks.

- Rule-based access control: A security model in which the system administrator defines the rules that to govern access to resource objects. Often these rules are based on conditions, such as time of day or location. It is not uncommon to use some form of both rule-based access control and role-based access control to enforce access policies and procedures.

- Attribute-based access control (ABAC): A methodology that manages access rights by evaluating a set of rules, policies and relationships using the attributes of users, systems and environmental conditions.

Use of Access Control

The goal of access control is to minimize the risk of unauthorized access to physical and logical systems. Access control is a fundamental component of security compliance programs that ensures security technology and access control policies are in place to protect confidential information, such as customer data. Most organizations have infrastructure and procedures that limit access to networks, computer systems, applications, files and sensitive data, such as personally identifiable information and intellectual property.

Access control systems are complex and can be challenging to manage in dynamic IT environments that involve on-premises systems and cloud services. After some high-profile breaches, technology vendors have shifted away from single sign-on systems to unified access management, which offers access controls for on-premises and cloud environments.

Implementing Access Control

Access control is a process that is integrated into an organization's IT environment. It can involve identity and access management systems. These systems provide access control software, a user database, and management tools for access control policies, auditing and enforcement.

When a user is added to an access management system, system administrators use an automated provisioning system to set up permissions based on access control frameworks, job responsibilities and workflows.

The best practice of "least privilege" restricts access to only resources that an employee requires to perform their immediate job functions.

A common security issue is failure to revoke credentials and access to systems and data when an individual moves into a different job internally or leaves the company.

Basic Access Authentication

HTTP supports the use of several authentication mechanisms to control access to pages and other resources. These mechanisms are all based around the use of the 401 status code and the WWW-Authenticate response header.

The most widely used HTTP authentication mechanisms are:

Basic	The client sends the user name and password as unencrypted base64 encoded text. It should only be used with HTTPS, as the password can be easily captured and reused over HTTP.
Digest	The client sends a hashed form of the password to the server. Although, the password cannot be captured over HTTP, it may be possible to replay requests using the hashed password.
NTLM	This uses a secure challenge/response mechanism that prevents password capture or replay attacks over HTTP. However, the authentication is per connection and will only work with HTTP/1.1 persistent connections. For this reason, it may not work through all HTTP proxies and can introduce large numbers of network round trips if connections are regularly closed by the web server.

Basic Authentication

If an HTTP receives an anonymous request for a protected resource it can force the use of Basic authentication by rejecting the request with a 401 (Access Denied) status code and setting the WWW-Authenticate response header as shown below:

```
HTTP/1.1 401 Access Denied

WWW-Authenticate: Basic realm="My Server"

Content-Length: 0
```

The word Basic in the WWW-Authenticate selects the authentication mechanism that the HTTP client must use to access the resource. The realm string can be set to any value to identify the secure area and may used by HTTP clients to manage passwords.

Most web browsers will display a login dialog when this response is received, allowing the user to enter a username and password. This information is then used to retry the request with an Authorization request header:

```
GET /securefiles/ HTTP/1.1

Host: www.httpwatch.com
```

```
Authorization: Basic aHR0cHdhdGNoOmY=
```

The Authorization specifies the authentication mechanism (in this case Basic) followed by the username and password. Although, the string aHR0cHdhdGNoOmY= may look encrypted it is simply a base64 encoded version of <username>:<password>.

Digest Access Authentication

Digest Access Authentication is one method that a client and server can use to exchange credentials over HTTP. This method uses a combination of the password and other bits of information to create an MD5 hash which is then sent to the server to authenticate. Sending a hash avoids the problems with sending a password in clear text, a shortfall of Basic Access Authentication.

Digest Access was originally defined in RFC 2069, and optional security enhancements were later added in RFC 2617 which should be considered the current standard if you wish to implement this method yourself.

Working with Digest Access Authentication

When working with Digest Access Authentication, it's the server who must make the first move when it discovers a client is trying to access a restricted area. There are a few values the server needs to provide as part of the WWW-Authenticate header that the client needs.

The server generates a value, referred to as nonce, which should be unique for each request. It's recommended this value be either Base64 or hexadecimal, specifically because it will be enclosed in double quotes and we want to ensure there are no double quotes in the string. The nonce will be used by the client to generate a hash to send back to the server.

In PHP, applying md5() to a unique string is generally sufficient.

```php
<?php

$nonce = md5(uniqid());
```

The next value needed by the client is opaque. This is another unique string generated by the server and is expected to be sent and returned by the client unaltered.

```php
<?php

$opaque = md5(uniqid());
```

The last value, realm, is just a string to display to users so they know which username and password they should provide. It's also used by the client to generate a hash to send back to the server.

```php
<?php

$realm = 'Authorized users of example.com';
```

All of these values are used to compose the WWW-Authenticate directive and send as a response to the client.

```php
<?php if (empty($_SERVER['PHP_AUTH_DIGEST']) {

  header('HTTP/1.1 401 Unauthorized');

  header(sprintf('WWW-Authenticate: Digest realm="%s", nonce="%s",

opaque="%s"', $realm, $nonce, $opaque));

  header('Content-Type: text/html');

  echo '<p>You need to authenticate.</p>';

  exit; }
```

When the client receives this response, it has to compute a return hash. It does so by concatenating the username, realm, and password and hashing the result with MD5 as follows:

1. Compute A1 as MD5("username:realm:password").

2. Compute A2 as MD5("requestMethod:requestURI").

3. Compute the final hash, know as "response", as MD5("A1:nonce:A2").

The client sends the response back to the server in an Authorization header and includes the username, realm, nonce, opaque, uri, and the computed response.

```
Authorization:    Digest    username="%s",    realm="%s",    nonce="%s",
opaque="%s", uri="%s", response="%s"'
```

Note that realm, nonce, and opaque are all returned to the server unchanged.

When the server receives the response, the same steps are taken to compute the server's version of the hash. If the computed hash and the received response hash values match, then the request is considered authorized. It looks something like this:

```php
<?php

$A1 = md5("$username:$realm:$password");

$A2 = md5($_SERVER['REQUEST_METHOD'] . ":$uri");

$response = md5("$A1:$nonce:$A2");
```

Of course, the user's password is never passed to the server. To perform authentication look-ups from a database then, the value of A1 can be stored. Keep in mind however the stored hash becomes invalid if you ever change your realm.

Improving on the Original Digest Access Spec

Now that you're familiar with the workings of Digest Access Authentication from RFC 2069, let's turn our attention to some of the enhancements that were added in 2617: qop, nc, and cnonce.

qop, or quality of protection, is specified in the WWW-Authenticate header and can have a value of "auth" or "auth-int". When no qop directive is found or when it is set to "auth", Digest Access is used for client authentication only – the default mode which you've seen so far. When set to "auth-int", an attempt is made to provide some level of integrity protection of the response as well and the client must also include the request body as part of the message digest. This allows the server to determine whether the request has been adulterated in transfer between the indented client and intended server.

The client nonce, or cnonce, is similar to nonce but is generated by the client. The cnonce figures into the response digest computed by the client and its original value is passed along to the server so that it can be used there to compare digests. This provides some response integrity and mutual authentication, in that both the client and server have a way to prove they know a shared secret. When the qop directive is sent by the server, the client must include a cnonce value.

The nonce count, nc, is a hexadecimal count of the number of requests that the client has sent with a given nonce value. This way, the server can guard against replay attacks.

With the enhancements, the computation of A2 and the response goes something like this:

```php
<?php if ($qop == 'auth-int') {

$A2 = md5($_SERVER['REQUEST_METHOD'] . ":$uri:" . md5($respBody));
} else {

$A2 = md5($_SERVER['REQUEST_METHOD'] . ":$uri");

}

$response = md5("$A1:$nonce:$nc:$cnonce:$qop:$A2");
```

Strengths and Weaknesses of Digest Access Authentication

Digest Access has some advantages over Basic Authentication, since Basic Authentication uses a clear-text exchange of username and passwords, which is almost the same as telling the world what your password is. Digest Access passes a hashed value and not the password itself, so it's much more secure than Basic Auth. The server nonce, which should be unique per request, will drastically change the computed hash on each new request, and the nc value provided by RFC 2617 is helpful at preventing replay attacks, whereby a malicious individual is able to intercept your request data and "replay" or repeat it as his own request.

There are a few weaknesses with Digest Authentication as well. When RFC 2617 replaced the original specification, the enhancements that were added to provide extra security measures between the client and server were made purely optional, and Digest Authentication will proceed in its original RFC 2069 form when not implemented.

Another problem is MD5 is not a strong hashing algorithm. All it takes is time and CPU to brute force the original value back to life. Bcrypt is preferable as it is more resilient against brute force attacks. There's also no way for a server to verify the identity of the requesting client when using Digest Access Authentication. This opens the possibility for man in the middle attacks, where a client can be led to believe a given server is really who he thinks it is, but ends up sending his login credentials to an unknown entity.

Your best bet when dealing with authentication is to use SSL and encrypt passwords using Bcrypt. You can use Basic Authentication or a home brewed authentication mechanism over SSL, but for situations where SSL is not possible for whatever reason, Digest Access is better than simple Basic Authentication and sending passwords in plain text over the public Internet.

Web Cache

Intelligent content caching is one of the most effective ways to improve the experience for your site's visitors. Caching, or temporarily storing content from previous requests, is part of the core content delivery strategy implemented within the HTTP protocol. Components throughout the delivery path can all cache items to speed up subsequent requests, subject to the caching policies declared for the content.

Caching is the term for storing reusable responses in order to make subsequent requests faster. There are many different types of caching available, each of which has its own characteristics. Application caches and memory caches are both popular for their ability to speed up certain responses.

Web caching, the focus of this guide, is a different type of cache. Web caching is a core design feature of the HTTP protocol meant to minimize network traffic while improving the perceived responsiveness of the system as a whole. Caches are found at every level of a content's journey from the original server to the browser.

Web caching works by caching the HTTP responses for requests according to certain rules. Subsequent requests for cached content can then be fulfilled from a cache closer to the user instead of sending the request all the way back to the web server.

Benefits

Effective caching aids both content consumers and content providers. Some of the benefits that caching brings to content delivery are:

- Decreased network costs: Content can be cached at various points in the network path between the content consumer and content origin. When the content is cached closer to the consumer, requests will not cause much additional network activity beyond the cache.

- Improved responsiveness: Caching enables content to be retrieved faster because an entire network round trip is not necessary. Caches maintained close to the user, like the browser cache, can make this retrieval nearly instantaneous.

- Increased performance on the same hardware: For the server where the content originated, more performance can be squeezed from the same hardware by allowing aggressive caching. The content owner can leverage the powerful servers along the delivery path to take the brunt of certain content loads.

- Availability of content during network interruptions: With certain policies, caching can be used to serve content to end-users even when it may be unavailable for short periods of time from the origin servers.

When dealing with caching, there are a few terms that you are likely to come across that might be unfamiliar. Some of the more common ones are below:

- Origin server: The origin server is the original location of the content. If you are acting as the web server administrator, this is the machine that you control. It is responsible for serving any content that could not be retrieved from a cache along the request route and for setting the caching policy for all content.

- Cache hit ratio: A cache's effectiveness is measured in terms of its cache hit ratio or hit rate. This is a ratio of the requests able to be retrieved from a cache to the total requests made. A high cache hit ratio means that a high percentage of the content was able to be retrieved from the cache. This is usually the desired outcome for most administrators.

- Freshness: Freshness is a term used to describe whether an item within a cache is still considered a candidate to serve to a client. Content in a cache will only be used to respond if it is within the freshness time frame specified by the caching policy.

- Stale content: Items in the cache expire according to the cache freshness settings in the caching policy. Expired content is "stale". In general, expired content cannot be used to respond to client requests. The origin server must be re-contacted to retrieve the new content or at least verify that the cached content is still accurate.

- Validation: Stale items in the cache can be validated in order to refresh their expiration time. Validation involves checking in with the origin server to see if the cached content still represents the most recent version of item.

- Invalidation: Invalidation is the process of removing content from the cache before its specified expiration date. This is necessary if the item has been changed on the origin server and having an outdated item in cache would cause significant issues for the client.

Content that can be Cached

Certain content lends itself more readily to caching than others. Some very cache-friendly content for most sites are:

- Logos and brand images
- Non-rotating images in general (navigation icons, for example)
- Style sheets
- General JavaScript files
- Downloadable Content
- Media Files

These tend to change infrequently, so they can benefit from being cached for longer periods of time.

Some items that you have to be careful in caching are:

- HTML pages
- Rotating images
- Frequently modified JavaScript and CSS
- Content requested with authentication cookies

Some items that should almost never be cached are:

- Assets related to sensitive data (banking info, etc.)
- Content that is user-specific and frequently changed

In addition to the above general rules, it's possible to specify policies that allow you to cache different types of content appropriately. For instance, if authenticated users all see the same view of your site, it may be possible to cache that view anywhere. If authenticated users see a user-sensitive view of the site that will be valid for some time, you may tell the user's browser to cache, but tell any intermediary caches not to store the view.

Locations Where Web Content is Cached

Content can be cached at many different points throughout the delivery chain:

- Browser cache: Web browsers themselves maintain a small cache. Typically, the browser sets a policy that dictates the most important items to cache. This may be user-specific content or content deemed expensive to download and likely to be requested again.

- Intermediary caching proxies: Any server in between the client and your infrastructure can cache certain content as desired. These caches may be maintained by ISPs or other independent parties.

- Reverse Cache: Your server infrastructure can implement its own cache for backend services. This way, content can be served from the point-of-contact instead of hitting backend servers on each request.

Each of these locations can and often do cache items according to their own caching policies and the policies set at the content origin.

Caching Headers

Caching policy is dependent upon two different factors. The caching entity itself gets to decide whether or not to cache acceptable content. It can decide to cache less than it is allowed to cache, but never more.

The majority of caching behavior is determined by the caching policy, which is set by the content owner. These policies are mainly articulated through the use of specific HTTP headers.

Through various iterations of the HTTP protocol, a few different cache-focused headers have arisen with varying levels of sophistication. The ones you probably still need to pay attention to are below:

- Expires: The Expires header is very straightforward, although fairly limited in scope. Basically, it sets a time in the future when the content will expire. At this point, any requests for the same content will have to go back to the origin server. This header is probably best used only as a fall back.

- Cache-Control: This is the more modern replacement for the Expires header. It is well supported and implements a much more flexible design. In almost all cases, this is preferable to Expires, but it may not hurt to set both values. We will discuss the specifics of the options you can set with Cache-Control a bit later.

- Etag: The Etag header is used with cache validation. The origin can provide a unique Etag for an item when it initially serves the content. When a cache needs to validate the content it has on-hand upon expiration, it can send back the Etag it has for the content. The origin will either tell the cache that the content is the same, or send the updated content (with the new Etag).

- Last-Modified: This header specifies the last time that the item was modified. This may be used as part of the validation strategy to ensure fresh content.

- Content-Length: While not specifically involved in caching, the Content-Length header is important to set when defining caching policies. Certain software will refuse to cache content if it does not know in advanced the size of the content it will need to reserve space for.

- Vary: A cache typically uses the requested host and the path to the resource as the key with which to store the cache item. The Vary header can be used to tell caches to pay attention to an additional header when deciding whether a request is for the same item. This is most commonly used to tell caches to key by the Accept-Encoding header as well, so that the cache will know to differentiate between compressed and uncompressed content.

The Vary header provides you with the ability to store different versions of the same content at the expense of diluting the entries in the cache.

In the case of Accept-Encoding, setting the Vary header allows for a critical distinction to take place between compressed and uncompressed content. This is needed to correctly serve these items to browsers that cannot handle compressed content and is necessary in order to provide basic usability. One characteristic that tells you that Accept-Encoding may be a good candidate for Vary is that it only has two or three possible values.

Items like User-Agent might at first glance seem to be a good way to differentiate between mobile and desktop browsers to serve different versions of your site. However, since User-Agent strings are non-standard, the result will likely be many versions of the same content on intermediary caches, with a very low cache hit ratio. The Vary header should be used sparingly, especially if you do not have the ability to normalize the requests in intermediate caches that you control (which may be possible, for instance, if you leverage a content delivery network).

How Cache-Control Flags Impact Caching

We previously mentioned how the Cache-Control header is used for modern cache policy specification. A number of different policy instructions can be set using this header, with multiple instructions being separated by commas.

Some of the Cache-Control options you can use to dictate your content's caching policy are:

- No-cache: This instruction specifies that any cached content must be re-validated on each request before being served to a client. This, in effect, marks the content as stale immediately, but allows it to use revalidation techniques to avoid re-downloading the entire item again.

- No-store: This instruction indicates that the content cannot be cached in any way. This is appropriate to set if the response represents sensitive data.

- Public: This marks the content as public, which means that it can be cached by the browser and any intermediate caches. For requests that utilized HTTP authentication, responses are marked private by default. This header overrides that setting.

- Private: This marks the content as private. Private content may be stored by the user's browser, but must not be cached by any intermediate parties. This is often used for user-specific data.

- Max-age: This setting configures the maximum age that the content may be cached before it must revalidate or re-download the content from the origin server. In essence, this replaces the Expires header for modern browsing and is the basis for determining a piece of content's freshness. This option takes its value in seconds with a maximum valid freshness time of one year (31536000 seconds).

- S-maxage: This is very similar to the max-age setting, in that it indicates the amount of time that the content can be cached. The difference is that this option is applied only to intermediary caches. Combining this with the above allows for more flexible policy construction.

- Must-revalidate: This indicates that the freshness information indicated by max-age, s-maxage or the Expires header must be obeyed strictly. Stale content cannot be served under any circumstance. This prevents cached content from being used in case of network interruptions and similar scenarios.

- Proxy-revalidate: This operates the same as the above setting, but only applies to intermediary proxies. In this case, the user's browser can potentially be used to serve stale content in the event of a network interruption, but intermediate caches cannot be used for this purpose.

- No-transform: This option tells caches that they are not allowed to modify the received content for performance reasons under any circumstances. This means, for instance, that the cache is not able to send compressed versions of content it did not receive from the origin server compressed and is not allowed.

These can be combined in different ways to achieve various caching behavior. Some mutually exclusive values are:

- No-cache, no-store, and the regular caching behavior indicated by absence of either.

- Public and private.

The no-store option supersedes the no-cache if both are present. For responses to unauthenticated requests, public is implied. For responses to authenticated requests, private is implied. These can be overridden by including the opposite option in the Cache-Control header.

Developing a Caching Strategy

In a perfect world, everything could be cached aggressively and your servers would only be contacted to validate content occasionally. This doesn't often happen in practice though, so you should try to set some sane caching policies that aim to balance between implementing long-term caching and responding to the demands of a changing site.

Common Issues

There are many situations where caching cannot or should not be implemented due to how the content is produced (dynamically generated per user) or the nature of the content (sensitive banking information, for example). Another problem that many administrators face when setting up caching is the situation where older versions of your content are out in the wild, not yet stale, even though new versions have been published.

These are both frequently encountered issues that can have serious impacts on cache performance and the accuracy of content you are serving. However, we can mitigate these issues by developing caching policies that anticipate these problems.

General Recommendations

While your situation will dictate the caching strategy you use, the following recommendations can help guide you towards some reasonable decisions.

There are certain steps that you can take to increase your cache-hit ratio before worrying about the specific headers you use. Some ideas are:

- Establish specific directories for images, css, and shared content: Placing content into dedicated directories will allow you to easily refer to them from any page on your site.

- Use the same URL to refer to the same items: Since caches key off of both the host and the path to the content requested, ensure that you refer to your content in the same way on all of your pages. The previous recommendation makes this significantly easier.

- Use CSS image sprites where possible: CSS image sprites for items like icons and navigation decrease the number of round trips needed to render your site and allow your site to cache that single sprite for a long time.

- Host scripts and external resources locally where possible: If you utilize JavaScript scripts and other external resources, consider hosting those resources on your own servers if the correct headers are not being provided upstream. Note that you will have to be aware of any updates made to the resource upstream so that you can update your local copy.

- Fingerprint cache items: For static content like CSS and JavaScript files, it may be appropriate to fingerprint each item. This means adding a unique identifier to the filename (often a hash of the file) so that if the resource is modified, the new resource name can be requested, causing the requests to correctly bypass the cache. There are a variety of tools that can assist in creating fingerprints and modifying the references to them within HTML documents.

In terms of selecting the correct headers for different items, the following can serve as a general reference:

- Allow all caches to store generic assets: Static content and content that is not user-specific can and should be cached at all points in the delivery chain. This will allow intermediary caches to respond with the content for multiple users.

- Allow browsers to cache user-specific assets: For per-user content, it is often acceptable and useful to allow caching within the user's browser. While this content would not be appropriate to cache on any intermediary caching proxies, caching in the browser will allow for instant retrieval for users during subsequent visits.

- Make exceptions for essential time-sensitive content: If you have content that is time-sensitive, make an exception to the above rules so that the outdated content is not served in critical situations. For instance, if your site has a shopping cart, it should reflect the items in the cart immediately. Depending on the nature of the content, the no-cache or no-store options can be set in the Cache-Control header to achieve this.

- Always provide validators: Validators allow stale content to be refreshed without having to download the entire resource again. Setting the Etag and the Last-Modified headers allow caches to validate their content and re-serve it if it has not been modified at the origin, further reducing load.

- Set long freshness times for supporting content: In order to leverage caching effectively, elements that are requested as supporting content to fulfill a request should often have a long freshness setting. This is generally appropriate for items like images and CSS that are pulled in to render the HTML page requested by the user. Setting extended freshness times, combined with fingerprinting, allows caches to store these resources for long periods of time. If the assets change, the modified fingerprint will invalidate the cached item and will trigger a download of the new content. Until then, the supporting items can be cached far into the future.

- Set short freshness times for parent content: In order to make the above scheme work, the containing item must have relatively short freshness times or may not be cached at all. This is typically the HTML page that calls in the other assisting content. The HTML itself will be downloaded frequently, allowing it to respond to changes rapidly. The supporting content can then be cached aggressively.

The key is to strike a balance that favors aggressive caching where possible while leaving opportunities to invalidate entries in the future when changes are made. Your site will likely have a combination of:

- Aggressively cached items.

- Cached items with a short freshness time and the ability to re-validate.

- Items that should not be cached at all.

The goal is to move content into the first categories when possible while maintaining an acceptable level of accuracy.

References

- What-is-web-server-and-different-types-of-web-servers: fastwebhost.in, Retrieved 12 April 2018

- Etag-header: logicbig.com, Retrieved 28 March 2018

- How-to-use-http-referer-3471200: lifewire.com, Retrieved 29 April 2018

- Everything-you-need-to-know-about-do-not-track-currently-featuring-microsoft-vs-google-and-mozilla: thenextweb.com, Retrieved 15 May 2018

- Access-control: searchsecurity.techtarget.com, Retrieved 17 March 2018

## 8

Proxy Servers

A proxy server is a computer system which works as an intermediary for handling requests from clients desiring resources from other servers. This is an important chapter, which will analyze in detail about the different proxy servers such as open proxy server, reverse proxy server, flash proxy, Java Anon proxy server, etc.

A proxy server, also known as a "proxy" or "application-level gateway", is a computer that acts as a gateway between a local network (e.g., all the computers at one company or in one building) and a larger-scale network such as the internet. Proxy servers provide increased performance and security. In some cases, they monitor employees' use of outside resources.

A proxy server works by intercepting connections between sender and receiver. All incoming data enters through one port and is forwarded to the rest of the network via another port. By blocking direct access between two networks, proxy servers make it much more difficult for hackers to get internal addresses and details of a private network.

Some proxy servers are a group of applications or servers that block common internet services. For example, an HTTP proxy intercepts web access, and an SMTP proxy intercepts email. A proxy server uses a network-addressing scheme to present one organization-wide IP address to the internet. The server funnels all user requests to the internet and returns responses to the appropriate users. In addition to restricting access from outside, this mechanism can prevent inside users from reaching specific internet resources (e.g., certain websites). A proxy server can also be one of the components of a firewall.

Proxies may also cache web pages. Each time an internal user requests a URL from outside, a temporary copy is stored locally. The next time an internal user requests the same URL, the proxy can serve the local copy instead of retrieving the original across the network, improving performance.

Types of Proxy Servers

Proxy servers are classified into several types based on purpose and functionality. Some of the most common types and their uses can be described as below:

Web Proxy is the most common type of proxy application, which responds to the user requests by accessing resources from cached web pages and files available on remote web servers. This facilitates quick and reliable access to data for local network clients. If the requested resource is not found in the cache, then a web proxy fetches the file from the remote server, and saves a copy in the cache before returning it to the client.

Transparent Proxy is mostly used for caching websites and overcoming simple IP bans. However, such proxies do not provide any user anonymity since user's original IP address is exposed. Transparent proxies are not specifically configured on the client computers.

Anonymous proxies do not hide the original IP address of the user; however, they provide adequate anonymity to most users. Anonymous proxies are easily detectable.

A distorting proxy, identifies itself as a proxy server, and modify the HTTP headers to disguise the original IP address.

Tunneling proxies are capable of passing client requests and return responses without making any modifications. These are also referred to as gateway proxies.

A forward proxy responds to client requests by retrieving data from a wide range of sources on the internet. It is also referred to as an Internet-facing proxy.

Open proxies belong to the category of forwarding proxy servers, which are accessible by any internet user since they can receive and return requests from any client computer. Meanwhile, anonymous open proxies are used for user anonymity to conceal the IP address.

Reverse proxies, also known as surrogates, usually receive requests from the Internet and forward them to internal network servers. A reverse proxy server forwards requests to one or more proxy servers, whose response is returned to the client computer, the user of which has no knowledge on the origin of the response.

Uses

Monitoring and Filtering

A content-filtering web proxy server provides administrative control over the content that may be relayed in one or both directions through the proxy. It is commonly used in both commercial and non-commercial organizations (especially schools) to ensure that Internet usage conforms to acceptable use policy.

A content filtering proxy will often support user authentication to control web access. It also usually produces logs, either to give detailed information about the URLs accessed by specific users, or to monitor bandwidth usage statistics. It may also communicate to daemon-based and/or ICAP-based antivirus software to provide security against virus and other malware by scanning incoming content in real time before it enters the network.

Many workplaces, schools and colleges restrict the web sites and online services that are accessible and available in their buildings. Governments also censor undesirable content. This is done either with a specialized proxy, called a content filter (both commercial and free products are available), or by using a cache-extension protocol such as ICAP that allows plug-in extensions to an open caching architecture.

Websites commonly used by students to circumvent filters and access blocked content often include a proxy, from which the user can then access the websites that the filter is trying to block.

Requests may be filtered by several methods, such as a URL or DNS blacklists blacklist, URLregex filtering, MIME filtering, or content keyword filtering. Some products have been known to employ content analysis techniques to look for traits commonly used by certain types of content providers. Blacklists are often provided and maintained by web-filtering companies, often grouped into categories (pornography, gambling, shopping, social networks, etc.).

Assuming the requested URL is acceptable, the content is then fetched by the proxy. At this point a dynamic filter may be applied on the return path. For example, JPEG files could be blocked based on flesh tone matches, or language filters could dynamically detect unwanted language. If the content is rejected then an HTTP fetch error may be returned to the requester.

Most web filtering companies use an internet-wide crawling robot that assesses the likelihood that a content is a certain type. The resultant database is then corrected by manual labor based on complaints or known flaws in the content-matching algorithms.

Some proxies scan outbound content, e.g., for data loss prevention; or scan content for malicious software.

Filtering of Encrypted Data

Web filtering proxies are not able to peer inside secure sockets HTTP transactions, assuming the chain-of-trust of SSL/TLS (Transport Layer Security) has not been tampered with.

The SSL/TLS chain-of-trust relies on trusted root certificate authorities. In a workplace setting where the client is managed by the organization, trust might be granted to a root certificate whose private key is known to the proxy. Consequently, a root certificate generated by the proxy is installed into the browser CA list by IT staff.

In such situations, proxy analysis of the contents of a SSL/TLS transaction becomes possible. The proxy is effectively operating a man-in-the-middle attack, allowed by the client's trust of a root certificate the proxy owns.

Bypassing Filters and Censorship

If the destination server filters content based on the origin of the request, the use of a proxy can circumvent this filter. For example, a server using IP-based geolocation to restrict its service to a certain country can be accessed using a proxy located in that country to access the service.

Web proxies are the most common means of bypassing government censorship, although no more than 3% of Internet users use any circumvention tools.

In some cases users can circumvent proxies, which filter, using blacklists using services designed to proxy information from a non-blacklisted location.

Logging and Eavesdropping

Proxies can be installed in order to eavesdrop upon the data-flow between client machines and the web. All content sent or accessed – including passwords submitted and cookies used – can be captured and analyzed by the proxy operator. For this reason, passwords to online services (such as webmail and banking) should always be exchanged over a cryptographically secured connection, such as SSL. By chaining proxies, which do not reveal data about the original requester, it is possible to obfuscate activities from the eyes of the user's destination. However, more traces will be left on the intermediate hops, which could be used or offered up to trace the user's activities. If the policies and administrators of these other proxies are unknown, the user may fall victim to a false sense of security just because those details are out of sight and mind. In what is more of an inconvenience than a risk, proxy users may find themselves being blocked from certain Web sites, as numerous forums and Web sites block IP addresses from proxies known to have spammed or trolled the site. Proxy bouncing can be used to maintain privacy.

Improving Performance

A caching proxy server accelerates service requests by retrieving content saved from a previous request made by the same client or even other clients. Caching proxies keep local copies of frequently requested resources, allowing large organizations to significantly reduce their upstream bandwidth usage and costs, while significantly increasing performance. Most ISPs and large businesses have a caching proxy. Caching proxies were the first kind of proxy server. Web proxies are commonly used to cache web pages from a web server. Poorly implemented caching proxies can cause problems, such as an inability to use user authentication.

A proxy that is designed to mitigate specific link related issues or degradations is a Performance Enhancing Proxy (PEPs). These typically are used to improve TCP performance in the presence of high round-trip times or high packet loss (such as wireless or mobile phone networks); or highly asymmetric links featuring very different upload and download rates. PEPs can make more efficient use of the network, for example by merging TCP ACKs(acknowledgements) or compressing data sent at the application layer.

Another important use of the proxy server is to reduce the hardware cost. An organization may have many systems on the same network or under control of a single server, prohibiting the possibility of an individual connection to the Internet for each system. In such a case, the individual systems can be connected to one proxy server, and the proxy server connected to the main server.

Translation

A translation proxy is a proxy server that is used to localize a website experience for different markets. Traffic from global audiences is routed through the translation proxy to the source website. As visitors browse the proxied site, requests go back to the source site where pages are rendered. Original language content in the response is replaced by translated content as it passes back through the proxy. The translations used in a translation proxy can be either machine translation, human translation, or a combination of machine and human translation. Different translation proxy implementations have different capabilities. Some allow further customization of the source site for local audiences such as excluding source content or substituting source content with original local content.

Accessing Services Anonymously

An anonymous proxy server (sometimes called a web proxy) generally attempts to anonymize web surfing. There are different varieties of anonymizers. The destination server (the server that ultimately satisfies the web request) receives requests from the anonymizing proxy server, and thus does not receive information about the end user's address. The requests are not anonymous to the anonymizing proxy server, however, and so a degree of trust is present between the proxy server and the user. Many proxy servers are funded through a continued advertising link to the user.

Access control: Some proxy servers implement a logon requirement. In large organizations, authorized users must log on to gain access to the web. The organization can thereby track usage to individuals. Some anonymizing proxy servers may forward data packets with header lines such as HTTP_VIA, HTTP_X_FORWARDED_FOR, or HTTP_FORWARDED, which may reveal the IP address of the client. Other anonymizing proxy servers, known as elite or high-anonymity proxies, make it appear that the proxy server is the client. A website could still suspect a proxy is being used if the client sends packets which include a cookie from a previous visit that did not use the high-anonymity proxy server. Clearing cookies, and possibly the cache, would solve this problem.

QA Geotargeted Advertising

Advertisers use proxy servers for validating, checking and quality assurance of geo-targeted ads. A geotargeting ad server checks the request source IP address and uses a geo-IP database to determine the geographic source of requests. Using a proxy server that is physically located inside a specific country or a city gives advertisers the ability to test geotargeted ads.

Security

A proxy can keep the internal network structure of a company secret by using network address translation, which can help the security of the internal network. This makes requests from machines and users on the local network anonymous. Proxies can also be combined with firewalls.

An incorrectly configured proxy can provide access to a network otherwise isolated from the Internet.

Cross-domain Resources

Proxies allow web sites to make web requests to externally hosted resources (e.g. images, music files, etc.) when cross-domain restrictions prohibit the web site from linking directly to the outside domains. Proxies also allow the browser to make web requests to externally hosted content on behalf of a website when cross-domain restrictions (in place to protect websites from the likes of data theft) prohibit the browser from directly accessing the outside domains.

Secondary Market Brokers

Secondary market brokers use web proxy servers to buy large stocks of limited products such as limited sneakers or tickets.

Implementations of Proxies

Web Proxy Servers

Web proxies forward HTTP requests. The request from the client is the same as a regular HTTP request except the full URL is passed, instead of just the path.

```
GET http://en.wikipedia.org/wiki/Proxy_server HTTP/1.1

Proxy-Authorization: Basic encoded-credentials

Accept: text/html
```

This request is sent to the proxy server, the proxy makes the request specified and returns the response.

```
HTTP/1.1 200 OK

Content-Type: text/html; charset UTF-8
```

Some web proxies allow the HTTP CONNECT method to set up forwarding of arbitrary data through the connection; a common policy is to only forward port 443 to allow HTTPS traffic.

Examples of web proxy servers include Apache (with mod proxy or Traffic Server), HAProxy, IIS configured as proxy (e.g., with Application Request Routing), Nginx, Privoxy, Squid, Varnish (reverse proxy only), WinGate, Ziproxy, Tinyproxy, RabbIT4 and Polipo.

SOCKS proxy

SOCKS also forwards arbitrary data after a connection phase, and is similar to HTTP CONNECT in web proxies.

Transparent proxy

Also known as an intercepting proxy, inline proxy, or forced proxy, a transparent proxy intercepts normal communication at the network layer without requiring any special client configuration. Clients need not be aware of the existence of the proxy. A transparent proxy is normally located between the client and the Internet, with the proxy performing some of the functions of a gateway or router.

RFC 2616 (Hypertext Transfer Protocol—HTTP/1.1) offers standard definitions:

"A 'transparent proxy' is a proxy that does not modify the request or response beyond what is required for proxy authentication and identification". "A 'non-transparent proxy' is a proxy that modifies the request or response in order to provide some added service to the user agent, such as group annotation services, media type transformation, protocol reduction, or anonymity filtering".

TCP Intercept is a traffic filtering security feature that protects TCP servers from TCP SYN flood attacks, which are a type of denial-of-service attack. TCP Intercept is available for IP traffic only.

In 2009 a security flaw in the way that transparent proxies operate was published by Robert Auger, and the Computer Emergency Response Team issued an advisory listing dozens of affected transparent and intercepting proxy servers.

Purpose

Intercepting proxies are commonly used in businesses to enforce acceptable use policy, and to ease administrative overheads, since no client browser configuration is required.

This second reason however is mitigated by features such as Active Directory group policy, or DHCP and automatic proxy detection.

Intercepting proxies are also commonly used by ISPs in some countries to save upstream bandwidth and improve customer response times by caching. This is more common in countries where bandwidth is more limited (e.g. island nations) or must be paid for.

Issues

The diversion / interception of a TCP connection creates several issues. Firstly the original destination IP and port must somehow be communicated to the proxy. This is not always possible (e.g., where the gateway and proxy reside on different hosts). There is a class of cross site attacks that depend on certain behaviour of intercepting proxies that do not check or have access to information about the original (intercepted) destination. This problem may be resolved by using an integrated packet-level and application level appliance or software, which is then able to communicate this information between the packet handler and the proxy.

Intercepting also creates problems for HTTP authentication, especially connection-oriented authentication such as NTLM, as the client browser believes it is talking to a server rather than a proxy. This can cause problems where an intercepting proxy requires authentication, then the user connects to a site, which also requires authentication.

Finally intercepting connections can cause problems for HTTP caches, as some requests and responses become uncacheable by a shared cache.

Implementation Methods

In integrated firewall / proxy servers where the router/firewall is on the same host as the proxy, communicating original destination information can be done by any method, for example Microsoft TMG or WinGate.

Interception can also be performed using Cisco's WCCP (Web Cache Control Protocol). This proprietary protocol resides on the router and is configured from the cache, allowing the cache to determine what ports and traffic is sent to it via transparent redirection from the router. This redirection can occur in one of two ways: GRE Tunneling (OSI Layer 3) or MAC rewrites (OSI Layer 2).

Once traffic reaches the proxy machine itself interception is commonly performed with NAT (Network Address Translation). Such setups are invisible to the client browser, but leave the proxy visible to the web server and other devices on the internet side of the proxy. Recent Linux and some BSD releases provide TPROXY (transparent proxy) which performs IP-level (OSI Layer 3) transparent interception and spoofing of outbound traffic, hiding the proxy IP address from other network devices.

Detection

There are several methods that can often be used to detect the presence of an intercepting proxy server:

- By comparing the client's external IP address to the address seen by an external web server, or sometimes by examining the HTTP headers received by a server. A number of sites have been created to address this issue, by reporting the user's IP address as seen by the site back to the user in a web page. Google also returns the IP address as seen by the page if the user searches for "IP".

- By comparing the result of online IP checkers when accessed using https vs http, as most intercepting proxies do not intercept SSL. If there is suspicion of SSL being intercepted, one can examine the certificate associated with any secure web site, the root certificate should indicate whether it was issued for the purpose of intercepting.

- By comparing the sequence of network hops reported by a tool such as traceroute for a proxied protocol such as http (port 80) with that for a non proxied protocol such as SMTP (port 25).

- By attempting to make a connection to an IP address at which there is known to be no server. The proxy will accept the connection and then attempt to proxy it on. When the proxy finds no server to accept the connection it may return an error message or simply close the connection to the client. This difference in behaviour is simple to detect. For example, most web browsers will generate a browser created error page in the case where they cannot connect to an HTTP server but will return a different error in the case where the connection is accepted and then closed.

- By serving the end-user specially programmed Adobe Flash SWF applications or Sun Java applets that send HTTP calls back to their server.

CGI Proxy

A CGI web proxy accepts target URLs using a Web form in the user's browser window, processes the request, and returns the results to the user's browser. Consequently, it can be used on a device or network that does not allow "true" proxy settings to be changed. The first recorded CGI proxy was developed by American computer scientist Richard Windmann on June 6, 1999.

The majority of CGI proxies are powered either by Glype or PHProxy, both written in the PHP language. As of April 2016, Glype has received almost a million downloads, whilst PHProxy still receives hundreds of downloads per week. Despite waning in popularity due to VPNs and other privacy methods, there are still several thousand CGI proxies online.

Some CGI proxies were set up for purposes such as making websites more accessible to disabled people, but have since been shut down due to excessive traffic, usually caused by a third party advertising the service as a means to bypass local filtering. Since many of these users don't care about the collateral damage they are causing, it became necessary for organizations to hide their proxies, disclosing the URLs only to those who take the trouble to contact the organization and demonstrate a genuine need.

Suffix Proxy

A suffix proxy allows a user to access web content by appending the name of the proxy server to the URL of the requested content (e.g. "en.wikipedia.org.SuffixProxy.com"). Suffix proxy servers are easier to use than regular proxy servers but they do not offer high levels of anonymity and their primary use is for bypassing web filters. However, this is rarely used due to more advanced web filters.

Tor Onion Proxy Software

Tor (short for The Onion Router) is a system intended to enable online anonymity. Tor client software routes Internet traffic through a worldwide volunteer network of servers in order to conceal a user's location or usage from someone conducting network surveillance or traffic analysis. Using Tor makes it more difficult to trace Internet activity, including "visits to Web sites, online posts, instant messages and other communication forms", back to the user. It is intended to protect users' personal freedom, privacy, and ability to conduct confidential business by keeping their internet activities from being monitored.

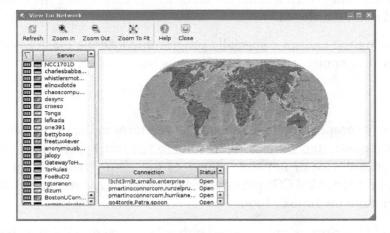

"Onion routing" refers to the layered nature of the encryption service: The original data are encrypted and re-encrypted multiple times, then sent through successive Tor relays, each one of which decrypts a "layer" of encryption before passing the data on to the next relay and ultimately the destination. This reduces the possibility of the original data being unscrambled or understood in transit.

The Tor client is free software, and there are no additional charges to use the network.

I2P Anonymous Proxy

The I2P anonymous network ('I2P') is a proxy network aiming at online anonymity. It implements garlic routing, which is an enhancement of Tor's onion routing. I2P is fully distributed and works by encrypting all communications in various layers and relaying them through a network of routers run by volunteers in various locations. By keeping the source of the information hidden, I2P offers censorship resistance. The goals of I2P are to protect users' personal freedom, privacy, and ability to conduct confidential business.

Each user of I2P runs an I2P router on their computer (node). The I2P router takes care of finding other peers and building anonymizing tunnels through them. I2P provides proxies for all protocols (HTTP, IRC, SOCKS).

The software is free and open-source, and the network is free of charge to use.

Proxy vs. NAT

Most of the time 'proxy' refers to a layer-7 application on the OSI reference model. However, another way of proxying is through layer-3 and is known as Network Address Translation (NAT). The difference between these two proxy technologies is the layer in which they operate, and the procedure to configuring the proxy clients and proxy servers.

In client configuration of layer-3 proxy (NAT), configuring the gateway is sufficient. However, for client configuration of a layer-7 proxy, the destination of the packets that the client generates must always be the proxy server (layer-7), then the proxy server reads each packet and finds out the true destination.

Because NAT operates at layer-3, it is less resource-intensive than the layer-7 proxy, but also less flexible. As we compare these two technologies, we might encounter a terminology known as 'transparent firewall'. Transparent firewall means that the layer-3 proxy uses the layer-7 proxy advantages without the knowledge of the client. The client presumes that the gateway is a NAT in layer-3, and it does not have any idea about the inside of the packet, but through this method the layer-3 packets are sent to the layer-7 proxy for investigation.

DNS Proxy

A DNS proxy server takes DNS queries from a (usually local) network and forwards them to an Internet Domain Name Server. It may also cache DNS records.

Open Proxy Server

Companies and ISPs often use caching in proxy servers to reduce the load on their networks. These proxy servers are often configured to proxy any port, with little regard to security. If nothing is blocking connections from the outside, it is possible to detect the vulnerable server by scanning the ports of a range of IP addresses.

Misconfigured Servers

Often, a proxy server is open because it has not been configured properly. Most of open proxy servers are not supposed to be public. The person that configured the server was not aware of the potential problems and security risks. It is very common to for a novice administrator to set up a proxy with access rights that allow anyone to connect. To close a proxy server it is necessary to force users to connect from one IP address or a range of IP addresses. An alternative is to require users to use a user name and password.

Honey Proxies

Everything that is done on or through the open proxy server can be logged and traced. A honey proxy or honey pot is an open proxy server intentionally deployed by security professionals to lure hackers and track their every move. A honey pot can also be installed by a hacker. A hacker can put a proxy server up on his, or a victim's computer and wait for a scanner to find it. Sending spam e-mail trough a honey pot proxy exposes the sender's activity. When a spammer uses the proxy to send bulk email, it is possible to collect the content of the spam and report the spammer to his ISP.

Security Risks

When you use an open proxy server, your computer is making a direct connection to another computer. You do not know who is in control of the remote computer. If you are using proxy servers from open proxy lists, you could be trusting your email messages, passwords or other sensitive information to a person running the server. Someone can be watching the unencrypted information you are transferring over the network.

Reverse Proxy Server

A reverse proxy is a server that sits in front of one or more web servers, intercepting requests from clients. This is different from a forward proxy, where the proxy sits in front of the clients. With a reverse proxy, when clients send requests to the origin server of a website, those requests are intercepted at the network edge by the reverse proxy server. The reverse proxy server will then send requests to and receive responses from the origin server.

The difference between a forward and reverse proxy is subtle but important. A simplified way to sum it up would be to say that a forward proxy sits in front of a client and ensures that no origin server ever communicates directly with that specific client. On the other hand, a reverse proxy sits in front of an origin server and ensures that no client ever communicates directly with that origin server.

Let's illustrate by naming the computers involved:

- D: Any number of users' home computers.

- E: This is a reverse proxy server.

- F: One or more origin servers.

Reverse Proxy Flow

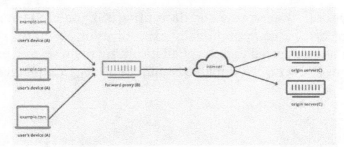

Typically all requests from D would go directly to F, and F would send responses directly to D. With a reverse proxy, all requests from D will go directly to E, and E will send its requests to and receive responses from F. E will then pass along the appropriate responses to D.

Benefits of a Reverse Proxy

- Load balancing - A popular website that gets millions of users every day may not be able to handle all of its incoming site traffic with a single origin server. Instead, the site can be distributed among a pool of different servers, all handling requests for the same site. In this case, a reverse proxy can provide a load balancing solution, which will distribute the incoming traffic evenly among the different servers to prevent any single server from becoming overloaded. In the event that a server fails completely, other servers can step up to handle the traffic.

- Protection from attacks - With a reverse proxy in place, a web site or service never needs to reveal the IP address of their origin server(s). This makes it much harder for attackers to leverage a targeted attack against them, such as a DDoS attack. Instead the attackers will only be able to target the reverse proxy, such as Cloudflare's CDN, which will have tighter security and more resources to fend off a cyber attack.

- Global Server Load Balancing (GSLB) - In this form of load balancing, a website can be distributed on on several servers around the globe and the reverse proxy will send clients to the server that's geographically closest to them. This decreases the distances that requests and responses need to travel, minimizing load times.

- Caching - A reverse proxy can also cache content, resulting in faster performance. For example, if a user in Paris visits a reverse-proxied website with web servers in Los Angeles, the user might actually connect to a local reverse proxy server in Paris, which will then have to communicate with an origin server in L.A. The proxy server can then cache (or temporarily save) the response data. Subsequent Parisian users who browse the site will then get the locally cached version from the Parisian reverse proxy server, resulting in much faster performance.

- SSL encryption - Encrypting and decrypting SSL (or TLS) communications for each client can be computationally expensive for an origin server. A reverse proxy can be configured to decrypt all incoming requests and encrypt all outgoing responses, freeing up valuable resources on the origin server.

Flash Proxy

Sometimes Tor bridge relays can be blocked despite the fact that their addresses are handed out only a few at a time. Flash proxies create many, generally ephemeral bridge IP addresses, with the goal of outpacing a censor's ability to block them. Rather than increasing the number of bridges at static addresses, flash proxies make existing bridges reachable by a larger and changing pool of addresses.

"Flash proxy" is a name that should make you think "quick" and "short-lived." Our implementation uses standard web technologies: JavaScript and WebSocket. (In the long-ago past we used Adobe Flash, but do not any longer.)

Flash Proxy is built into Tor Browser. In fact, any browser that runs JavaScript and has support for WebSockets is a potential proxy available to help censored Internet users.

Working of Flash Proxy

In addition to the Tor client and relay, we provide three new pieces. The Tor client contacts the flash proxy facilitator to advertise that it needs a connection. The facilitator is responsible for keeping track of clients and proxies, and assigning one to another. The flash proxy polls the facilitator for client registrations, then begins a connection to the client when it gets one. The transport plugins on the client and the relay broker the connection between WebSockets and plain TCP.

A Sample Session May Go Like This:

1. The client starts Tor and the client transport plugin program (flash proxy-client), and sends a registration to the facilitator using a secure rendezvous. The client transport plugin begins listening for a remote connection.

2. A flash proxy comes online and polls the facilitator.

3. The facilitator returns a client registration, informing the flash proxy where to connect.

4. The proxy makes an outgoing connection to the client, which is received by the client's transport plugin.

5. The proxy makes an outgoing connection to the transport plugin on the Tor relay. The proxy begins sending and receiving data between the client and relay.

From the user's perspective, only a few things change compared to using normal Tor. The user must run the client transport plugin program and use a slightly modified Tor configuration file.

Cupcake

Cupcake is an easy way to distribute Flash Proxy, with the goal of getting as many people to become bridges as possible.

Cupcake can be distributed in two ways:

- As a Chrome or Firefox add-on (turning your computer into a less temporary proxy)

- As a module/theme/app on popular web platforms (turning every visitor to your site into a temporary proxy)

Java Anon Proxy Server

Java Anon Proxy Server or JAP (called JonDo in the scope of the commercial) JonDonym anonymous proxy servers - AN.ON remains free of charge) makes it possible to surf the internet anonymously and unobservably.

Without Anonymization, every computer in the internet communicates using a traceable Address. That means:

- the website visited,

- the internet service provider (ISP),

- and any eavesdropper on the internet connection

can determine which websites the user of a specific computer visits. Even the information which the user calls up can be intercepted and seen if encryption is not used. JAP uses a single static address which is shared by many JAP users. That way neither the visited website, nor an eavesdropper can determine which user visited which website.

Working of Java Anon Proxy Server

Instead of connecting directly to a webserver, users take a detour, connecting with encryption through several intermediaries, so-called Mixes. JAP uses a predetermined sequence for the mixes. Such a sequence of linked mixes is called a Mix Cascade. Users can choose between different mix cascades.

Since many users use these intermediaries at the same time, the internet connection of any one single user is hidden among the connections of all the other users. No one, not anyone from outside, not any of the other users, not even the provider of the intermediary service can determine which connection belongs to which user. A relationship between a connection and its user could only be determined if all intermediaries worked together to sabotage the anonymization.

The intermediaries (mix providers) are generally provided by independent institutions, which officially declare, that they do not keep connection log files or exchange such data with other mix providers. JAP shows the identity and number of organisations in each Mix cascade in detail, and verifies this information by cryptographic means. The users are thus able to selectively choose trustable mix cascades.

Architecture of the Anonymization Service

The structure of the JAP anonymization service is shown schematically in the following diagram. It consists of the following components:

- JAP Client program installed on the user's computer.

- Mixes Anonymizing intermediaries, which mix the data streams of various users together.

- InfoService a separate service which provides meta-information about the available mixes (that is, mix cascades), number of users currently using the mix cascades, and the current load on the mix provider.

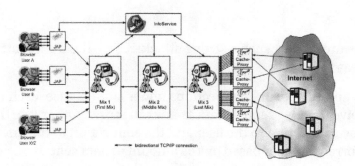

When you start the JAP client program, JAP first connects to the InfoService to check if the program version is still current. If the version of the program is no longer compatible with the software of the mix, the user is automatically offered a program update, since otherwise the JAP service could no longer be used.

In the next step, JAP registers with the first mix station of the chosen mix cascade. A permanent network connection between JAP and the first mix station remains until logoff.

On installation of JAP, the user already configured the web browser so that each packet of data sent goes through JAP instead of directly to the internet. JAP encrypts the data and sends it to the first mix station. The first mix station then mixes the data with that of other users and sends it to the second mix station which passes it on to the third mix station which decrypts and sends the data through a cache proxy to the internet.

Each mix carries out cryptographic operations on the message so that the JAP-encrypted data is only readable when it's gone through the proper mixes in the proper order. That way it's insured, that an eavesdropper either only receives unreadable (encrypted) data or can no longer determine the sender. In order for it to work correctly, only one mix in the cascade need be trusted not to inform the eavesdropper as to the method of message mixing.

Weaknesses of JAP

Our goal is to create an anonymization service, which is secure against an attacker of almost any strength. There should be only two restrictions:

1. A mix in the cascade should not be controlled by an attacker and should not work together with an attacker.

2. The attacker should not control all other users. (An attacker could then observe a single real user, since the real user is alone and the attacker would know that all data which the attacker himself didn't send came from that single user.)

Otherwise the attacker is allowed to try anything. He can listen to all connections, attempt to manipulate or delete any data, or even insert new data messages.

Possible Attacks

JAP is not yet secure against such a strong attacker. Two theoretical attack possibilities against JAP are as follows:

If an attacker keeps all network connections under surveillance, each user would have to send and receive exactly as much data as any other user. Otherwise the attacker, who observes both the connection to the user and the connection to the internet after the final mix, could correlate a user based on the amount of data sent. If one user sends more data than all the other users, that's most likely the one communicating with another user who is receiving large amounts of data at the end of the cascade.

Currently, we can't defend against such an attack for various reasons. Users have different connection speeds and varying amounts of activity at any given time. If one wanted to achieve an equivalent behavior pattern among all users who have the same connection speed, yet maintain a similar quality of service, the mixes would require many times the current bandwidth. In addition, any disturbance experienced by a single user would have an effect on all other users, since they would have to wait until the one user with the connection problems sent as much data as all the rest.

A second theoretically possible attack is as follows: Currently a single attacker could simulate multiple users by simply starting several JAP client programs. That way, he could at least fool the remaining users into believing in a higher amount anonymity than what is really available. If the attacker would furthermore block all real users except for one, the anonymity of that single remaining user would be completely eliminated.

To prevent this kind of attack, it would be necessary to authenticate every user at login, for example with a digital signature. With a pay-based service, such an attack could at least be made very expensive for the attacker.

There are currently still other attacks possible, since the planned basic functions are not yet completely implemented. On the other hand, an attacker would have to be relatively strong in order to succeed in any attack.

Ziproxy

Ziproxy is Web proxy server, but rather than cache content the way Web proxies like Squid do, it's designed to compress the content that it fetches from the Web before forwarding it to the Web client. It can be useful for serving mobile devices like handheld Internet tablets that cannot take full advantage of high-resolution, high-quality images, or where the browser client is running over a mobile data plan where speed is low and bytes are expensive.

Ziproxy can compress images to lower quality (smaller) JPEG or JPEG 2000 files and can optimize HTML and CSS content for size before compressing it with gzip. While JPEG 2000 images require a lot of computational power to decode, they can also be substantially smaller than PNG or normal JPEG images. Many Web browsers automatically decompress content that is gzip-encoded, so the end user cannot tell that compression of HTML and CSS was used.

The commands to build Ziproxy are shown below:

```
$ tar xjf /FromWeb/ziproxy-2.5.2.tar.bz2

$ cd ./ziproxy-2.5.2/

$ ./configure --with-jasper

$ make

$ sudo make install

$ su -l

# cp -av etc/ziproxy /etc

# chown -R root.root /etc/ziproxy
```

Ziproxy comes with an init.d file that can be used to start the daemon, but there are a few issues with starting Ziproxy using this script. For one, the path for Ziproxy is hard-coded, and the script will not find the binary if it is installed in /usr/local. The most serious issue is that it will start Ziproxy as the root user. To remedy these problems, we created a new user to run the program, then edited the script, as you'll see below. In the line calling printf, I removed the "g" from the original call to gprintf. Wrapping the invocation of Ziproxy with the su command is the major change.

```
# useradd ziproxy

# mkdir /var/log/ziproxy

# chown ziproxy.ziproxy /var/log/ziproxy

# cp /.../ziproxy-2.5.2/etc/init.d/ziproxy /etc/init.d

# vi /etc/init.d/ziproxy

...

PID_FILE=/var/tmp/ziproxy.pid

ZIPROXY=/usr/local/bin/ziproxy

...
```

```
printf "Starting %s: " "${PROGNAME}"

...

su -c "${ZIPROXY} -d -c ${ZIPROXY_CONF} >${PID_FILE}" ziproxy

...

# /etc/init.d/ziproxy start
```

You can run Ziproxy either through xinetd or as a standalone daemon. we'll run it standalone, as this usually yields improved performance. Any client connection filtering that might be done via xinetd can be performed through packet filtering and the use of SSH port forwarding to securely access Ziproxy from the Internet.

Before starting Ziproxy, take a look at its configuration file in /etc/ziproxy/ziproxy.conf. The first options allow you to set the port and address that Ziproxy will bind to. The OnlyFrom option lets you set an IP address or a contiguous range of IP addresses (in the form begin.IP-end.IP) that are allowed to access the proxy. If OnlyFrom is not specified then any client that can connect to the address and port that Ziproxy is bound to will be served. If you are using Ziproxy to provide a Web proxy to mobile devices, one option is to set OnlyFrom=127.0.0.1 and use SSH port forwarding to connect to the Web proxy.

Many of the options in ziproxy.conf specify which image formats will be (re)compressed, which formats an image can be compressed into, and how aggressively to set image compression parameters. In the above two use cases, you are unlikely to want images to be compressed into JPEG 2000 format for a device that has minimal system RAM and a relatively slow CPU, such as those of an Internet tablet. On the other hand, you might want all images to be recompressed into JPEG 2000 if you are planning to access the proxy from a relatively fast laptop over a slow link.

The image compression quality settings can change depending on how large (in pixels) in image is. It is more likely that you would like a better-quality image for the larger images on a Web page. As an added bonus, if you specify negative values, then the image is first converted to gray-scale and then compressed with the given quality. You must specify four values for quality settings to use for images up to 5,000, 50,000, and 250,000 pixels, and all images larger than these sizes; for example, ImageQuality={17,20,23,25}. If you want to compress in JPEG 2000, use the JP2ImageQuality keyword instead.

By default Ziproxy will try to recompress PNG, JPG, and GIF images. You can turn off recompression for an image format with boolean options like ProcessJPG. If you want to recompress to JPEG 2000 instead of normal JPEG if possible then set Process-ToJP2=true. Conversely, if you want to recompress any JPEG 2000 image to normal JPEG, set ForceOutputNoJP2=true. There's also a small collection of options relating to how to compress JPEG 2000 images.

To affect text compression set Gzip=true/false; the default is true. If your client does not handle gzip compressed content or you are accessing the proxy of SSH and prefer to use SSH compression, you might turn this off. The Compressible={"shockwave","foo"} option lets you tell Ziproxy to compress a nominated list of other data types as well.

A collection of options starting with the Process prefix let you specify if HTML, CSS, and JavaScript files should be modified en route. These options might make the content slightly smaller, but they are marked as experimental.

You can set a limit (in bytes) on the size of a file that Ziproxy will try to (re)compress using the MaxSize option.

Setting the ImageQuality values to all negative to force Ziproxy to convert all images to gray-scale provides a quick visual indication as to which images have been treated by Ziproxy on a Web page. Inspecting the log files during initial testing against linux.com and slashdot.org didn't show much compression being performed by Ziproxy; in fact, the only things that were gray-scale were non-Flash adverts.

Further Refinement

One method of using Ziproxy is to configure it to only allow connections from local host. Clients would then use SSH port forwarding to access the proxy, connecting a port of the client machine to the machine that is running Ziproxy. Although SSH has the -C option to compress communications, by turning off SSH compression and relying on Ziproxy for compression you will achieve better compression, particularly of image files. Generic compression (ssh -C uses gzip) is not going to be able to compete with JPEG for images.

Advertisements and safe browsing checks can comprise the lion's share of bytes transferred when viewing a Web site. Even if you get rid of ads with software like Adblock Plus, Ziproxy can offer substantial reductions in the number of bytes transferred to your client. How effective Ziproxy is at compressing CSS and HTML content depends on how well the Web sites that you browse already take advantage of client supported implicit compression. While gzip compression of HTML and CSS saves bytes in a manner that an end user cannot detect, the configuration options also let you tailor how many artifacts are introduced into your images in order to save even more bytes.

References

- Thomas, Keir (2006). Beginning Ubuntu Linux: From Novice to Professional. Apress. ISBN 978-1-59059-627-2

- Proxy-server: iplocation.net, Retrieved 29 June 2018

- "Transparent Proxy Definition". ukproxyserver.org. 1 February 2011. Archived from the original on 1 March 2013. Retrieved 14 February 2013.

- Open-proxy-servers: postcastserver.com, Retrieved 31 March 2018

- "Layering". Performance Enhancing Proxies Intended to Mitigate Link-Related Degradations. IETF. June 2001. p. 4. sec. 2.1. doi:10.17487/RFC3135. RFC 3135. Retrieved 21 February 2014.

- Reverse-proxy: cloudflare.com, Retrieved 11 May 2018

- "Socket Capable Browser Plugins Result In Transparent Proxy Abuse". The Security Practice. 9 March 2009. Retrieved 14 August 2010.

- Faster-web-page-load-times-mobile-devices-ziproxy: linux.com, Retrieved 19 April 2018

- Zwicky, Elizabeth D.; Cooper, Simon; Chapman, D. Brent (2000). Building Internet Firewalls (2nd ed.). p. 235. ISBN 978-1-56592-871-8.

Permissions

Index

www.ingramcontent.com/pod-product-compliance
Lightning Source LLC
Jackson TN
JSHW052203130125
77033JS00004B/206